Terry,
Enjoying our
friendship —
in "dharma"
and in life!
love,
Lauren

9/02

THE FEELING BUDDHA

By the same author

A GUIDE TO PSYCHODRAMA
BEYOND CARL ROGERS
ZEN THERAPY

THE FEELING BUDDHA

A BUDDHIST PSYCHOLOGY OF CHARACTER, ADVERSITY AND PASSION

David Brazier

Fromm International
New York

First Fromm International Edition, 1998

Copyright © David Brazier 1997

All rights reserved under International and Pan-American copyright convention. Published in the United States by Fromm International Publishing Corporation, New York. First published by Constable, London, 1997.

LIBRARY OF CONGRESS CATALOGING-IN-PUBLICATION DATA

Brazier, David.
  The Feeling Buddha / David Brazier.
   p. cm.
  Includes bibliographical references and index.
  ISBN 0-88064-198-3
  1. Four Noble Truths. I. Title.
  BQ4230.B73 1998   98-28558
  294.3'420427--dc21   CIP

10 9 8 7 6 5 4 3 2 1
Manufactured in the United States of America

Contents

Part 4 · Character

Part 5 · Path

Acknowledgements

I have been helped in the production of this book by the loving support of my wife Caroline who has shared many hours of discussion of the material presented here, and the unstinting co-operation of my mother who also proof read the draft text. Many people have taught me Dharma, some famous and some unknown, and all have contributed something to shaping what has emerged between these covers. By no means all of them would agree with what is written here – I take responsibility for the contents of this book entirely upon myself – but I wish particularly to acknowledge the contribution to my Buddhist education made by the late Reverend Master Jiyu Kennett Roshi, by Dhyana Master Thich Nhat Hanh, by Sister Annabel Laity, by the late Chogyam Trungpa Rimpoche, by Achaan Virodhammo Bhikkhu and by innumerable members of the sanghas of the Community of Interbeing, Samye Ling Monastery, Throssel Hole Buddhist Monastery, The Forrest Sangha, the Pure Land Fellowship and the Amida Trust. I would also like to acknowledge the co-operation and encouragement to put pen to paper which I have received from Carol O'Brien and from Robin Baird-Smith.

Technical terms

I have done my best to eliminate Sanskrit words from the main text. Where they may aid the more specialised reader they are given in end notes. Even there, however, I have dispensed with diacritical marks. The reason for this policy is that it assists the process whereby a range of Buddhist terms is gradually becoming accepted into the English language, a language from which such marks are absent. The scholar will have no difficulty knowing what word I am referring to. A few Sanskrit terms remain in the main text. These are not many, but they are very significant. They fall into the following categories. Firstly, there are words like nirvana, karma and buddha which have already found a place in the English language. Secondly, there are the four words *dukkha, samudaya, nirodha* and *marga*, the reinterpretation of which is a key feature of the story of the book. Thirdly, there are a very small number of other foreign words like *samadhi* (Sanskrit) and *koan* (Japanese) which it would be more confusing to translate than to leave alone. Generally, where a non-English word is used it appears in italic on first usage and in regular type thereafter. There is a glossary at the back of the book for the reader's convenience.

Part 1

The Birth of Wisdom

No Pearl without Grit

We live in a world that is uniquely adapted to our needs. Above our heads the sky is perpetually rearranging its inspiring beauty. Here on the ground earth provides everything that the human race could require. Sounds, colours and tastes abound. We are remarkably fortunate or, at least, we could be, if it were not for certain of our propensities that introduce seemingly insuperable difficulties into this Garden of Eden. Life is not easy. Even in the midst of collective plenty, people may live individual lives of desperation and emptiness. Suffering and affliction are part of what it means to be alive.

The problem of suffering has always been the inspiration for human passion in all its range from the highest achievements of art, spirit and culture through to the most sordid degradations of war, squalor and addiction. Often we turn to religion or spirituality in the hope of a magically reassuring answer. The Way taught by the Buddha[1], however, begins with recognition of the reality that this wonderful life is also full of innumerable difficulties. We meet with obstacles and opposition. We also carry a lot of suffering and trouble about within ourselves.

Generally, Buddhism is presented as the way to overcome suffering. It is formulated as a remedy for all the pain of life. This book does not present Buddhism that way. The message of the Buddha, as you will find it in these pages, is not that of escape, but of how to live a noble and satisfying life, in which the affliction and trouble are as essential as the grit is to the pearl. I will not tell you here that the enlightenment of the Buddha is a state in which you will no longer experience distress. Many things in the Buddha's own life were distressing enough and I do not think that his enlightenment was such as to make him insensitive to them.

What I will do is to take you through the very first teaching that the Buddha gave. This is called 'The Setting in Motion of the Wheel of the Dharma'. *Dharma* is the word for the Buddha's teaching. So this book is a reflection upon the way the Buddha first explained his enlightenment when it was very new and fresh. The 'Setting in Motion' is thus an immensely rewarding discourse to reflect upon if one is interested in knowing what the Buddha offered and continues to offer to the world.

The problem of suffering is at the heart of all spiritual enquiry. In the monotheistic religions, Christianity, Islam and Judaism, there is always the difficult question: if God is good and God made the world, why did he make it so full of suffering? Why do children die? Why do we see armies burn innocent civilians, volcanoes asphyxiate villages, and animals eat one another alive? If disaster has struck down somebody we love and we are a believer in God, we may well ask: does he not care? How can God be called good when the world works like this? This problem of suffering has been at the heart of the question of faith for westerners for a long time. Unable to resolve it, many in the past hundred years have abandoned religion and pinned their hopes on the advance of science as a new route to human salvation.

Science, however, offers no better answers. Science will tell us how to do something, but not what to do. Science will just as readily supply us with the means to exterminate one another more efficiently as it will provide the means for us to feed one another. In itself, science is indifferent. The old god may have been open to question on the issues of whether he cared for his creatures or not. The new god, science, certainly does not care. Nor should it, particularly. Science is not a god, however much modern people may want to make it into one. The continuous application of science does not solve moral dilemmas. It does not address the struggle of the human heart.

Since neither the old god nor the new one seem to have the answer to the question of suffering, an increasing number of people have turned toward Buddhism, looking for a new formula. In this book I will introduce the Buddha's teaching by showing how it is centrally concerned with the question of living meaningfully in an afflicted world. I will also, in passing, reveal some of the ways in which Buddhism has been commonly misunderstood.

Every one of us has our story, and in that story there is suffering. Suffering is terrible, but a story without suffering is dull. The word 'spirit' has something to do with the way we encounter adversity. A spiritual life should be a spirited one. The planet on which we live is beautiful, a kind of paradise. Yet, in the midst of the most amazing blessings, grief falls like an unexpected hail storm on a summer day, or like a winter of unexpected severity. Nor is it just the moment of injury that hurts. The pain goes on. The mother who loses a child may mourn for the rest of her life. The losses and separations that we all encounter mark us and make us. Nobody is truly mature who has not suffered.

When we suffer we may look for someone to blame. Blame breeds feuds. Feuds breed more and more suffering. Much of the social structure of our civilisation has grown up historically to inhibit the terribly destructive effects of feuding and bitterness. This external structure, however, is often inadequate to the task. It is not easy to induce a gathering of human beings to live in real harmony, either with their neighbours or with their natural surroundings.

Not only do we blame our neighbours, we also blame ourselves. This can be even more destructive. The anguish and shame which people carry within themselves become hard to bear and so we use the mechanisms of psychological repression. We stop looking at what we have done to ourselves. We paper over our hurt with a fabric of half-truths. Lives become shallow and unauthentic. Society as a whole begins to become a charade.

Modern psychology has fathomed many of the mechanisms of mental repression and this is to the good. Knowing a bit about how something works, however, does not stop it happening. As the world becomes more and more crowded, we need to know more than how the mechanisms work. We need some guidance on how to live. It is in this climate that Buddhism has an appeal to many western people who have no family history of eastern spirituality.

Buddhism is not a superficial palliative. The not uncommon interpretation of Buddhism which takes its message to be that, if you are sufficiently non-attached, you will be immune to grief because you will not care enough about anything to grieve over it, will not do. If the Buddhist message were simply that you will not suffer if you do not care, it would hardly have proved the inspiration that it has in the history of human civilisation.

No. The Buddha did not teach escape. The Buddha taught noble living. Noble living is not pain-free but it is meaningful. Indeed, it is the very opposite of escape. The noble person is not a coward. The Buddha taught that a radical change is possible in the way a person lives their life and sees their world. This radical change is called enlightenment. Enlightenment is a cathartic experience. One should not be deceived by the word into thinking this is a cerebral affair. Enlightenment is heart-felt. Enlightenment experiences may be minor or massive. A person who sincerely seeks true spirituality may well have a number of major enlightenment experiences in a lifetime and a great many minor ones. They cannot be contrived and con-trolled because their very nature is that they are a break through into new authenticity.

What should the seeker of enlightenment do? Fearlessly look into the seat of the trouble. Where the grief is strongest, the doubt most disturbing, the turmoil most opaque, the ignorance most dark – that is the place where enlightenment will break through. Lotuses only grow in swamps. When most people attempt this, however, they simply thrash about getting nowhere. Then they resort to the idea that enlightenment is so far off that they cannot be expected to attain it and settle for the moderate cultivation of a few virtues as a down payment on what they expect to be a very slow repayment plan. It takes a long time to redeem one's soul by such a method. In fact it does not work. Nonetheless, if one cannot summon the necessary energy, perhaps it is better than nothing.

Then, one day, fate takes a hand. Suddenly, the things we had relied upon are threatened. Our loved one dies or, worse, turns out to be unfaithful. Or the bargain we had made with fate comes apart. Fate cannot be bargained with. A man came to see me, telling me of the terrible burdens he was labouring under. These were real enough. His wife had died ten years earlier. He had given up a promising career to dedicate himself to his children. In consequence he was now impoverished. Not only that. One child developed a degenerative physical disease. A second had recently been diagnosed schizophrenic. A third, he suspected, was taking drugs. The fourth was attempting to study for school-leaving exams while family stress raged around her. He felt exhausted.

This man was near his limit. His afflictions were real enough. Actually, objectively, the situation had been just as bad for many years. Why was this the crisis time? Because he had inwardly set himself to cope until the children left home. He had paced himself to manage a difficult situation by holding on to the belief that it would end at a certain date and he would then be free. Now it was becoming rapidly obvious that fate was not going to keep its side of the bargain. At least two of the children, perhaps three, were not going to fly the nest at the appointed time.

A similar kind of magical thinking often occurs when someone near to us is dying. We think: 'if I am just good enough, or caring enough (or whatever) they will not die.' We make the effort and they die anyway. Then we despair and lose faith. Actually, it is this moment of despair when we have the greatest opportunity for real enlightenment. That is the point where reality breaks through our self-deception and gives us a chance to enter the real world where all real satisfactions are to be found. Enlightenment lies beyond despair.

Similarly, the spiritual practitioner, pleasant in every way, who is regularly making instalments upon a place in nirvana or heaven, by meditating, prostrating, praying, reciting, making offerings and performing acts of charity, and regarded by all as a solid member of the congregation, is an excellent person who is still, nonetheless, deluded. His opportunity for enlightenment will come when he realises that his strategy is not going to work and has been ill-founded from the beginning. Unfortunately, it might not happen until he is on his death bed. Such a waste.

In Buddhism there is no God to call to account. Suffering simply is. There is no denying it and there is no one to blame. Whoever may be to blame – perhaps even ourselves in a former manifestation – is no more. The present is what it is. There is no escape. We do our best to escape, nonetheless. The Buddha himself went to the utmost lengths to escape the suffering he carried within himself. He abandoned his wife and child. He rejected his birthright. He left teacher after teacher. He practised self-mortification to the limit. He was very hard on himself and difficult to live with at that time. Nothing could throw off the haunting knowledge that his mother died giving birth to him: the pain of knowledge that lay in his heart and that could never be undone. The important thing that the Buddha discovered was that none of his attempts to escape worked. Enlightenment came after he despaired of them. It came in the midst of the most terrible night of his life in which he did not get a wink of sleep because all the torments that were within him assailed him from every side. There are plenty of sanitised accounts of the night of the Buddha's enlightenment which paint us a picture of dignified triumphal procession with the Buddha winning every encounter. The reality, however, must have been a nightmare.

In the end, he found himself grown up and alone. If this seems like a terrible prospect to you, stop reading now. It is, however, the gateway to all real satisfaction. In his new awakening he experienced the most profound joy there is. In his aloneness he found himself in communion with all beings everywhere.

· 2 ·

The Courage of Ordinary Lives

BODILY ILLS

Yesterday Ella was talking to me about what life is like for her. Ella has a disease of the spine which restricts her movement and makes many everyday tasks difficult. Every day she has some pain. Things that most people take for granted, like reaching out to take something down from a shelf, are very hard and sometimes impossible. Living with recurring pain is not pleasant. It is very tiring. It also means that a good deal of thought has to be invested in how to do things and in assessing how much it is reasonable to expect the body to do.

Ella is a young woman. She explains to me how it is not really the physical pain and the inconvenience, unpleasant as these are, that distress her most. When she looks at her condition soberly, she sees that she has a deep sense that she should not be like this. It is this sense of not being as she should be that causes the greatest unease. Having a disease of this kind at her age involves a kind of shame.

'Sometimes I need to do some simple thing like pick up a piece of paper off the floor, and I know I cannot do it. Or if I can do it, it is going to be difficult and painful. And there may be somebody close by who could easily pick up the piece of paper for me. But I feel ashamed to ask.'

At this point we both smile. We both recognise the so human quality of this situation. We both know how difficult it is to accept infirmities and how the embarrassment of our condition may be far harder to cope with than the practical problems of the condition itself.

For Ella, the embarrassment of not being as fit and able as

she would like to be makes her disease far harder to bear. She has the inevitable suffering of pain and restriction and then she has the additional anguish of embarrassment which seems to twist inside her. To say that the pain of disease is physical and that the pain of embarrassment is psychological is a conventional way of speaking but, in fact, embarrassment is felt in a very physical way. Body and mind are by no means as readily separated as our conventions of speech suggest.

'There was a time when I felt completely defeated. I just gave up on everything. I felt like a complete failure. I had been used to being fit and able to do all the normal things. I liked to be outdoors and go for long walks. As the disease took hold, I tried really hard not to let it affect my life, but after a time I just had to admit that it was winning. I suppose you would say that I became depressed. I did not think of it as depression, but I just could not bring myself to do anything. Even the things I could still do seemed pointless.'

It is clear that Ella has come through the worst time because she is now active again within the limits imposed by her condition.

'I gradually learned some acceptance. I am far from having completely overcome the psychological difficulty of it, but I do accept more. I have discovered meditation and I feel a great determination to do that. Probably I will not manage to keep it going as consistently as I would like, but somehow it feels very important to sit. I can sit, even if I can't run any more.'

Soon after my discussion with Ella, I was talking to Tom and Rachel. Tom is quite a lot older than Ella. His hearing is not as good as it used to be. Rachel has a very soft voice. Tom asked her to speak louder. The way he said it was a bit abrupt, probably reflecting the embarrassment that he felt in having to ask. Rachel said that she would try, but I could tell by her tone of voice that she was a little offended by Tom's abrupt intervention which cut across what she was trying to say. The volume of her voice did increase very slightly for a short time, but after a sentence or two it was as quiet as before. I could see that Tom was feeling too awkward to ask again. He was trying hard to follow what Rachel was saying, but I am sure that he only got a small part of it. For my part, I was unsure how much he had understood so, when Rachel had finished I tried, in my reply, to incorporate some repetition of her main points. I knew that Tom would have a better chance of hearing my stronger voice. Nonetheless, I felt the embarrassment that we all shared.

Then Tom spoke. He did not really respond to what had been the topic of conversation up to that point, but rather shifted the focus to a story about a friend of his who is going blind. At the end of his story, Tom remarked that he did not know which was worse, to go blind or to go deaf. Our conversation continued for some time on the topic of social and personal attitudes to infirmity and gradually our shared embarrassment eased away as we came to understand each other better.

In our modern society we are constantly assailed by images of health, beauty and well-being which are held up as desirable ideals in advertising and films. This is not, however, a phenomenon of our society alone. If we go to Greece, or even to a museum of Greek artefacts, and look at the statues that the ancient peoples made, we see again images of perfection. I try to imagine how a person in ancient Greece may have felt as he or she made a secret comparison between their own physique and that of the gods, goddesses and athletes that they saw so skilfully represented in marble. The art of portraiture throughout the ages has been, to a large degree, the art of flattery or envy.

Nor is it just physical form which we are told should match a standard of perfection. We are also constantly encouraged to live our lives in certain ways and, in particular, to acquire certain things which we are somehow convinced will bring us happiness.

AND MENTAL ANGUISH

Peter came to see me because he feels his life is meaningless. He is not unusual in this respect.

Many people feel that dreadful inner emptiness that philosophers call by the French word *ennui*.

'I ought to be happy. I have a good wife and successful children. I own my own comfortable house. At work I have achieved a senior position in the profession which I always wanted to work in and my income is more than adequate for my needs. Somehow, it does not make me happy.'

Peter feels as though he has been tricked. In his mind, he has done all the things which should yield happiness, but this desired prize has not arrived. He feels as though he has kept his half of a bargain and the other party has not kept their word. Who the other party is, he is not sure. These are just things you learn to take for granted.

I listen and Peter tells me more about his life. He confesses that, in order to mitigate the feelings of loneliness, he sometimes takes drugs and quite often drinks more alcohol than he should. He has also sometimes felt drawn to women other than his wife and got involved in 'mild flirtations'. I sense that he is shy of telling me the real extent of some of his 'misbehaviour' but I get a clear sense of how it springs from a deep-seated desperation. Finally, he says that he has no spiritual path or faith and I can tell that he senses that this fact is somehow related to the core of his problem.

Helen, on the face of it, has a very different problem from Peter. Her life is 'a mess'. She is divorced. She works in a job that she hates. 'I only do it for the money.' She has a bulimic behaviour pattern. When she feels anxious she eats excessively, cramming food into her body. The food she chooses for this purpose is not nutritious wholefood, but is mostly things that she knows to be bad for her. When she has filled herself up with chocolate and doughnuts, she feels so ashamed and dirty that she goes to the bathroom and makes herself sick. She does this most days at least once and sometimes more often.

There was a time when Helen was more like Peter. Before her divorce, her life looked, on the surface at least, more conventional. Even now, to an observer who did not know her secrets, she would look like a normal citizen and a casual observer might think her quite happy and successful. She is competent at her job and can be quite assertive in public situations. To be divorced nowadays is not unusual and if people know that she dislikes her job – well, that is not uncommon either. The 'mess' is hidden, just like the vomit which she only brings up behind a locked door.

Where Peter had grown up thinking that he had a right to happiness, if only he behaved in the right way and achieved the right things, Helen never believed that she would or could be happy. Although she has done many of the same things as Peter – pursuing a career, getting married, earning money, buying herself a comfortable house – really she deeply doubts that any of this can make her happy. However, she does not want to put these doubts to the test. So over and over again she embarks upon a course of action that convention suggests should bring satisfaction but, before it has a chance to demonstrate that it will fail to do so, she aborts the experiment.

When we see this pattern, we see that it applies to many aspects of her life that might otherwise seem quite separate. She eats a bar of chocolate. Chocolate is supposed to be a treat and eating it is supposed to make you happy. So she eats a lot of it, but then immediately vomits. Unconsciously, she is avoiding having it proved to her that chocolate does not make you happy. We might think that eating chocolate is a small thing and getting married is a big thing. In Helen's life, however, the same pattern applies. Marriage is supposed to make a woman happy, so she got married. Deep inside she doubts that marriage can make her happy. She does not want to have to experience having this doubt proved true, so she finds herself compulsively acting in ways that ensure that the marriage never has a chance of success from the very beginning. It is as though she vomits the marriage up as soon as she has swallowed it.

Perhaps Helen is slightly wiser than Peter in that she has not been taken in by the promise that worldly success will make her happy. But nor is she really willing to face the implications of what she knows.

So Helen has arrived at a kind of unhappy equilibrium. Her habit of grasping and rejecting fills up all her time, takes all her energy and ensures that the intuition that she has about the emptiness of mundane life can never really be tested. She can continue to believe that all will be well when she overcomes her 'problem' so long as she does not overcome it.

Deep down Helen knows that eating chocolate will not make her happy. Chocolate can give us pleasure, however. If I eat a modest amount of chocolate slowly, savouring each piece, it tastes very good. The same is true of eating a piece of bread. Recently I completed a ten-day fast. I did this at a Buddhist monastery and, while I was fasting, I compared experiences with one of the nuns who had also practised fasting. She said that sometimes she fasted by eating two pieces of thinly cut dry bread each day. You chew the bread for a long time, until it becomes completely liquid in your mouth. 'It tastes delicious,' she said.

The difference between the nun eating dry bread and enjoying it and Helen eating chocolate and getting sick is basically that the nun is completely focused in the present moment. She is just eating the bread. When Helen eats chocolate she hardly tastes the chocolate at all. In the same way, Peter does not really participate in his marriage or his job or his nice house. The 'happiness' he thinks is his due lies beyond these things for him. In his mind they are a means to an end, not the end in itself.

Helen and Peter are both in flight from the suffering in their lives rather than enjoying the actual pleasures that are available to them. It is not really that the suffering is unbearable, in the sense of being acutely painful, like a severe burn might be. In important respects, the psychological pain of being in flight from the present reality of one's life can be far more disabling than the effect of such a burn. Ella's life was disrupted by her illness, but it was disrupted far more by the embarrassment and shame she felt about it and, as she has reached a greater acceptance of her physical condition, she has become happier again, like a flower opening in the sunshine after the storm clouds have passed.

· 3 ·

Misunderstanding Buddhism

When I first encountered Buddhism, I was a very serious young man. I decided that if I was going to practise Buddhism properly, I should read what the Buddha himself said. I did not understand the languages of India, so I was dependent upon translations. Fortunately, about that time, I lived in a house in which there was a very good library which included an extensive collection of translations of the traditional Buddhist texts. I started at the beginning and read and read. Much of what I read inspired me. I was amazed to find that here were books, some written down more than two thousand years ago, that spoke to me so directly and relevantly. It was very exciting. Many of the texts, called *Sutras*, record the talks and conversations of the Buddha. Others, called *Vinaya*, talked about the conduct of the members of the Buddhist community and told stories about how this or that way of behaving became established, usually as a result of a mistake that someone made. A third collection, called *Abhidharma*, are more difficult to read, being more technical. The Abhidharma books are actually the world's first psychology textbooks. I found it all fascinating.

I discovered that the books I had been reading were originally written in a language called Pali and that there was another large collection of texts in addition to these. This second collection had been written in a different language called Sanskrit. The Sanskrit works were later translated into Chinese and Tibetan and many of the original Sanskrit versions were lost. Initially, I found the books in this second collection much more difficult to understand, but after persevering with them for some years I gradually came to love them deeply.

This present short book does not provide space to say

everything. In any case there are many books about Buddhist teaching that you can read. I must say, however, that over the thirty years that have passed since I began my Buddhist studies, I have frequently come to the point of realising, to my shame, that there were quite fundamental points that I had for many years completely misunderstood. I had taken them to mean something rather different from what I now believe the Buddha really intended. In addition to this, I came to realise that there were a number of different perspectives among those who had translated the Buddha's words into English and that these perspectives affected their choice of words and so affected the way that the reader understood or failed to understand the Buddha's meaning.

On top of this, it seems that the Buddha's teachings were probably not actually written down until about three or four hundred years after he lived. In those days before written communication had become normal, people were trained to remember things well. Nonetheless, there must have been a good deal of scope for distortion to enter into the teaching over such a period. Such distortion would be, in some respects, systematic. The people who learned the teachings off by heart would recite them to audiences. The members of the audience would ask questions. I think there would be a natural tendency for the reciters to emphasise or elaborate the aspects of the teaching which went down well with the audience. There would be a tendency for the prevailing culture of the society to affect the way the teaching was given and the way it was construed. I realised, therefore, that I was reading the Buddha's teachings through at least three filters. The first was the cultural distortion which entered in before the texts were written down. The second was the attitudinal distortion introduced by translators. The third filter was provided by my own limitations.

In addition to rereading more carefully, two things in particular have helped me to reach a clearer understanding. The first of these has been attempting to put the teachings into practice. The second has been listening to other people talking about their experience of real life. These two things have for me been closely connected with each other. As a result of reading the Buddhist teachings, I quickly came to the conclusion that a change of lifestyle and career was called for. Consequently I have spent most of my adult life working as a social worker, Buddhist minister and psychotherapist. In all these roles I have been in a privileged position to listen to people's stories. As hundreds of people have shared with me the reality of their lives, I have gradually come to understand the Buddha's teachings more deeply. I have also come to appreciate the relevance of the Buddha's teachings to the arts of psychotherapy and social work and to some of the dilemmas of modern society.

I would like to share a little of my struggle to understand what the Buddha was really saying. I hope that this book will help you and me better to understand the Buddha's intention. Having said this, I must add that the conclusions I have come to are far from orthodox. The way I now construe the Buddha's meaning is, in some important respects, very different from what was presented to me in the first books I read about Buddhism. You may well have read some of these books yourself. If so, then you will find some surprises in the pages ahead. You may find what is written here exciting and liberating, or you may find that you strongly disagree.

SETTING THE WHEEL TURNING

The beginning in studying Buddhism, for me as for many other people, was the talk that the Buddha gave at the Isipatana Deer Park near Benares shortly after he was first enlightened: the 'Setting in Motion the Wheel of Dharma'.[1] This talk contains the essence of the Buddha's message. In the years of teaching that followed the essential points remained the same. This talk has, therefore, continued to be regarded by Buddhists as the heart of the matter for two and a half thousand years. When words are held in reverence for many centuries, they may benefit many people and there is no doubt that the Buddha's message of compassion has been a wonderful inspiration to millions of people. It is also true however that, simple as it is, there are important aspects of the Buddha's teaching which many people find difficult to understand and I now believe that for many years my own understanding of it was quite faulty.

This book explains what I now believe the Buddha actually meant by his teaching at Isipatana. I will indicate some of the key implications this teaching has for spiritual practice, for understanding human psychology and for the conduct of daily life. I will also say a little about how the talk at Isipatana is commonly understood and highlight the differences between that orthodox version and the interpretation presented here. Sometimes the difference between the two interpretations is subtle. Sometimes it is major. Before we get into a discussion of the content of the talk, however, we need to review the context in which it was given.

Cutting Mother Earth

The Buddha was troubled by the suffering in the world. In this fact he was just like us. It is not just that we do not like pain. It is also that the existence of suffering seems to offend us in a deep way. The feeling we have about suffering affects our sense of who we are and our attitude toward ourselves: whether we feel confident or whether we are dogged by shame and depression. This revulsion at suffering seems to be very basic to the way people are made. For the Buddha, like ourselves, this feeling was powerful and deep. The Buddha differed from us, if at all, only in the degree of courage with which he investigated the meaning of this problem.

The Buddha's personal name was Siddhartha Gautama. When Siddhartha was a little boy, he had a very privileged life. In chapter two, we saw how many people work hard to achieve the kind of circumstances that they believe will make them happy, only to be disappointed. For Siddhartha, everything was already at hand. He was provided with everything he could possibly desire. His father ardently wanted him to become successful in the world and brought him up to be accustomed to luxury and power. None of this, however, yielded him the happiness that we all seek. He had everything from the beginning, yet he still suffered. Riches and self-indulgence do not bring happiness. Perhaps Siddhartha learned this lesson earlier than most people because of his circumstances.

There was a particular source of suffering for Siddhartha that he could do nothing about and that pleasures endlessly multiplied were unable to erase. This was the fact that his mother had died giving birth to him. The story says that Siddhartha was born from her side. This may be simply a literary device to indicate the Buddha's kinship with a number of gods who were believed to have been born in this way, or it may be an indication that some kind of Caesarean operation was performed. However that may be, Queen Mahamaya died a few days after the birth. Knowing that someone has died that you may live is not the sort of knowledge that it is easy to ignore. When this person is your own mother, the situation is particularly poignant. This knowledge was a suffering that the Buddha could not escape.

Siddhartha grew up to be a sensitive child. By this I do not mean that he was sickly. He seems to have been a vigorous youth who excelled in martial arts. In particular, he became a skilled archer. Nonetheless, he had a deep compassion for animals and people. We are told of a dispute he had with his cousin, Devadatta. The two boys had been out playing and Devadatta had shot down a swan flying overhead. Siddhartha found the fallen bird and saw that it was still alive. He wanted to keep the bird to nurse it back to health. We can imagine the argument that ensued: 'I shot it down. It's mine.' 'I found it. It's mine.' So the boys quarrelled. Adults were called upon to arbitrate. Siddhartha's appeal was upheld when he said, 'Should not the bird belong to the one who wants to save its life and not to the one who wants to kill it?' The adults were impressed by this argument and gave the bird to Siddhartha. The rivalry between Devadatta and Siddhartha was to continue for most of their lives.

Later Siddhartha was to recount how the most crucial incident of his childhood occurred when he was nine. In the spring he was taken to the ploughing festival. This was a very important day for the Shakya people who were agriculturalists. On this day, the ploughing season began. The king, Siddhartha's father, would ceremonially cut the first furrow with a special plough. It was the occasion for a great spring festival and everybody was celebrating. Siddhartha was taken along by his nurse maids to watch his father perform the all important symbolic act of making the first cut in the ground.

As Siddhartha watched, what this sensitive child saw was the beautiful earth being cut open: cut open in order that the people might grow crops and so live; cut open just as, perhaps, he knew that his mother had been cut open to give him life. He saw insects turned up by the plough, ejected from their homes. He saw worms cut into pieces. He saw the birds descend and eat the little creatures squirming on the broken soil. He saw that in this cutting there was much suffering. He felt the suffering himself. He felt a great urge to remove himself from this painful spectacle. He slipped away from his nurse maids and went to sit under a tree. Later they came looking for him and found that he had gone into a deep state of concentration. As he reflected upon what he had witnessed he was unaware of their approach or of them observing him. This was the first time, he entered into the kind of intense rapture we call *samadhi*.

So Siddhartha grew up with a deep concern about the meaning of suffering in his heart. He knew that he was alive because his mother had died. He knew that people were only able to feed at the expense of the cutting of the earth. He felt the unavoidability of much suffering acutely. He went out from the palace and he saw people who were sick and he learned how nobody is immune to sickness. He saw how people grow old and how nobody is able to avert doing so if they live long. And if they do not live, then they die and this too is an affliction, both for the person who dies and for those who grieve. Siddhartha was certainly sensitive enough to grieve. The great mass of suffering in the world seemed to weigh upon him.

Siddhartha became aware that there were some people, wandering holy men, who seemed to have achieved at least some degree of freedom from this burden which weighs upon the heart. He discovered that there were great teachers, men like Alara Kalama and Uddaka Ramaputta, who were said to be able to overcome the sufferings of this life. He decided that he had to go and study with these teachers. So, while still in his twenties, he left home and went away to study the spiritual practices. He studied for many years and became expert in all the different meditations and austerities that these teachers taught to him. The basic theory behind these teachings was that the body is the source of all our suffering and so the body must be overcome. Overcoming the body was attempted through asceticism or what in western spirituality is called penance. This means going against what the body seems to want – asserting mind over matter. Siddhartha tested this approach to its very limits. He eventually fasted to the very threshold of death and collapsed in a ditch, being too weak to raise himself.

AN ACT OF SIMPLE KINDNESS

At this point a milk maid called Sujata happened to be passing by. She was on her way to make an offering to the forest gods and was carrying a milk and rice dish given to her by her mother for this purpose. Then she saw the monk fallen on the ground: a man in his weakness, his bones sticking out and his strength all gone. She offered the milk rice to the monk and he accepted it.

Over the next few days she continued to come and offer him food and gradually nursed him back to health. Later the Buddha was to teach that there was a great deal more merit in making offerings of food to sincere spiritual seekers than in giving offerings to gods. No doubt that teaching, like all his teachings, was rooted in his own personal experience.

There are many ways in which we could interpret this event. Why did Siddhartha give up his fast at this point? I am inclined to think that the simple kindness of Sujata touched him deeply. She had, in her innocence, a lesson for him that was just as profound as everything he had learned from the famous yogins he had studied with. She was willing to respond to simple human need with direct compassion. In the thinking of the time, what she did was probably sacrilegious. She gave the offering which was meant for the god to a man in the ditch. She did it without a second thought and continued to act in the same spirit until the man was recovered. She exemplified simple compassion, undistorted by metaphysical ideas.

Siddhartha had a profound realisation at this point. He understood clearly that happiness was not going to be achieved by torturing the body, any more than it had been found by indulging it. He had tried both these routes and carried them to their extreme. Neither worked. Happiness resided in the simple kindness of Sujata who was willing to respond to need when she saw it.

A few nights later Siddhartha sat in meditation beneath a tree. He knew that he had already understood some very important things and sensed that he was on the point of a crucially important breakthrough. I think we should not under-estimate the emotional element in this situation. No doubt Siddhartha had had many important ideas. What was necessary was not just to find the right thought, but to understand in his bones. Sujata did not teach him a doctrine. She touched his heart.

He meditated all night and watched everything that arose in his mind. Many fantasies and emotions assailed him: some violent, some lustful, some terrifying and some tempting. It is both reassuring and illuminating to discover that someone who was only a matter of hours away from becoming a buddha was afflicted by all the same mental perversions that the rest of us suffer from whenever we stop censoring ourselves. Not only did he experience all these emotions, thoughts and fantasies flooding into his mind and body, he also realised how they arose and experienced how insubstantial and impermanent they were. He recognised their relationship to the affliction which he sought to understand. This was a deeply cathartic experience. He saw how the mind worked, how the body gets impelled into behaviour by the mind, how a person thus builds an unauthentic identity, and how the continuing defence of this identity enslaves and hurts us.

The Buddha-to-be realised that the arising of such impulses could not be prevented. By seeing their true nature, however, he could remain undefeated by them. He saw that each such impulse was like a seed which, if it were encouraged to grow, could take over and blight one's life. Although he could not prevent them from arising, there was something he could do. By understanding their source and their effect he could change their consequences. They could be converted.

This experience of arising and transformation formed itself into a dramatic vision in his mind. It was as though the forces of death were assailing him, each carrying its own special weapon, each trying to get its hook into his flesh. As each one charged toward him, he would see its true nature and it would transform into something beautiful – a rainbow, a shower of petals, a smiling face. This vision made a deep impression upon him and inspired his teaching for many years to come. He realised that it represented a deep truth. He reached down and touched the earth and, we are told, the earth shook.

Siddhartha felt a profound connection with the earth. The earth was his witness. She was like a mother to him as she really is to all of us. He reached enlightenment sitting upon her unbroken skin and it was natural for him to reach out to her at the moment of complete understanding. At the moment of enlightenment the fatal rend in the flesh of the world was healed.

· 5 ·

Introducing the Four Noble Truths

Siddhartha was now a buddha, which is to say, he had woken up to an authentic way of living and he is able to bring this possibility to others. The new Buddha travelled to a place near Benares where some of his former companions, a group of five ascetics, were staying and delivered to them the talk to which we have already referred, the 'Setting in Motion of the Wheel of the Dharma'. In this talk he presents the kernel of his message in the form of 'Four Noble Truths'. This is the defining moment in Buddhist history.

One of the ascetics, Kondañña, as he listened, was immediately filled with great elation. He suddenly saw what he had not realised before. He, too, was enlightened. Kondañña knew with complete certainty that what the Buddha was saying was right and he saw how this teaching completely resolved the struggle that had been going on in him for many years.

The other ascetics were greatly impressed. They did not reach the same complete conviction as Kondañña, but they realised that the Buddha was on to something and they were deeply influenced by the transformation they saw in Kondañña. They all asked to become disciples. Similar scenes were to be repeated many times. The Buddha travelled and offered his teaching to many other spiritual practitioners. They were all struggling with the basic question of the meaning of suffering, but were trapped in the prevailing philosophies of the day. These philosophies said that happiness comes either through one's own efforts in subduing the body or through persuading the gods by praise, sacrifice and ritual to smile upon us. The Buddha's teaching rejected both these paths as futile.

The Buddha also taught ordinary people. Some of these

33

ordinary people also understood quickly what the Buddha was saying. Some did not. Many became disciples. Some were inspired enough to change their lifestyle and follow the Buddha's teaching. These people were called 'stream-enterers'. The Buddha was confident that stream-enterers would, in due course, reach complete enlightenment. Stream-enterers were those who had faith enough to start putting the teaching into practice in their own lives. Some were monks. Some were lay people. Stream-enterers had faith and this gave their life meaning and direction. The enlightened were beyond faith: they did not just believe what the Buddha said, they knew it was true from their own experience.[1] People who have persistently struggled with the deep questions of life are ripe for deep understanding, like Kondañña. In enlightenment, faith and personal knowledge merge, yielding an experience of radiant confidence.

The enlightenment of Kondañña occurred immediately. He did not study as a disciple of the Buddha for years and years before this event. The first hearing of the Dharma was enough. There are many other stories in the Buddhist books of people who were ripe becoming enlightened straight away. What the Buddha taught is not necessarily something that takes a long time to understand. It is not something that only those who have been through special initiations and followed a prescribed syllabus of study for decades can penetrate. What the Buddha taught is available here and now to anyone willing to go directly to the heart of the matter. It is something which any sincere person can test out for themselves from their own experience. The majority of people, like the other four ascetics, will not usually understand the full depth of the Buddha's message, but they may still recognise that there is something very important here and this may lead them to change their lives in important ways. Others awaken immediately.

FLOWING ONE WAY

So what did the Buddha say at Isipatana? If we can understand this we will, like Kondañña, have penetrated to the heart of the matter and may feel the joy of liberation in our hearts. Now we are getting close to the core of our task. At this point you may like to read the translation of the Buddha's talk which is provided as an appendix at the end of this book. Or you may prefer to continue as we unwind the thread of the Buddha's teaching, and leave reading the text itself for later.

First the Buddha set the scene by saying that he had learned that neither the extreme of self-indulgence nor the extreme of self-mortification work. They do not fulfil their promise. Each may seem to offer a route to the end of suffering, but neither succeeds in doing so. In fact, they actually make the suffering in our lives worse. Self-indulgence leads to all sorts of trouble. Over-eating fosters disease and shortens life and, since all food production involves some destruction of life, causes many other beings to suffer unnecessarily. Sexual misbehaviour leads to all manner of grief and emotional pain. A life devoted to the pursuit of entertainment is wasteful and unproductive and, in any case, just leads to boredom. Alcohol and drugs yield short-term pleasures, but they dull our minds, damage our bodies and dislocate our lives. Self-indulgence does not yield happiness.

On the other hand, self-mortification does not yield happiness either. Although we may learn some very important things through such practices as fasting, living in solitude, and doing without sleep, carrying a penitential lifestyle to an extreme leads to exhaustion rather than release and is, in any case, inherently painful.

The Buddha says: 'Avoiding these two extremes I have realised the Middle Path.' This, he says, is a path of vision, understanding, calm, insight, enlightenment and nirvana. It is a path of Right View, Right Thought, Right Speech, Right Action, Right Livelihood, Right Effort, Right Mindfulness, and Right Samadhi. It is the nature of this Middle Path that we have to understand.

The Buddha does not, however, at this point go into an explanation of vision, understanding, calm, insight, enlighten-ment and nirvana, nor of the eight limbs of the path, important as all these elements clearly are in his teaching. He begins with a more fundamental explanation of what the enlightened life essentially consists of. He does so very succinctly by spelling out the Four Noble Truths. In my explanation so far, everything I have said will be common knowledge to Buddhists in general and widely agreed upon.

What then are these four essentials that the Buddha called noble and true? In Sanskrit, they are called *dukkha, samudaya, nirodha,* and *marga.* I will try to keep the usage of Sanskrit terms to a minimum, but I hope that you will be willing to get used to reading these four terms, since it is so central to the task of this book to explore what exactly the Buddha meant by each of them. Very loosely, at this stage, we may say that *dukkha* means 'affliction'. The First Truth is that affliction a fact of life. *Samudaya* means 'arising'. The Second Truth is that in this world of afflictions, something arises in us. *Nirodha* means 'containment'. The Third Truth is that what arises can be contained and that such containment is essential to constructive living. *Marga* means 'path' or 'track'. The Fourth Truth sets out the characteristics of such a constructive, enlightened life. The rest of this book is devoted to explaining the implications of what the Buddha here proposes to us.

Before going on, however, let us pause a moment to see where we are heading. The Buddha revealed a Middle Path consisting of Right View, Right Thought and so on. The word here translated as 'Right' actually has the implication of 'all flowing (or moving) in one direction'. The term 'middle' could be read a number of ways. What I think the Buddha had in mind was something like the middle current in a river. When we look at a river, we see that the current in the middle flows swiftly. The water is powerful because it all flows in one direction. It is unified. The water at the edges tends just to go round in circles. It is not caught up in the mainstream. The Middle Way of the Buddha is not middle in the sense of an anaemic compromise. It is middle in the sense of being the mainstream of life, all flowing together, not wasting energy and not divided against itself. The Buddha set in motion a movement of people who, notwithstanding their diversity, were unified within themselves and with one another. They did not engage in self-defeat. It was this which gave the Buddhist movement its dynamism and momentum. It is this that we must recreate for the sake of our world today.

People are unified and flowing together when they are authentic, genuine or congruent. The Middle Way is a state of optimum mental health, free of self-defeating views, self-defeating thoughts, self-defeating actions, self-defeating speech, self-defeating modes of livelihood, self-defeating effort, self-defeating memories and self-defeating visions. In particular, our efforts to avoid the reality of affliction and passion are self-defeating. Siddhartha himself had spent many years in a self-defeating quest for the end of suffering. In the process he had multiplied his suffering a thousandfold and brought much distress to his family and friends along the way. Self-defeating behaviour just puts us into a backwater, just as it had put him into a ditch. Now he saw that there is an authentic way of living that is not self-defeating. When we adopt this Middle Way, we leave the backwater and enter the main current of the river.

Kondañña, like the Buddha, had pursued the same self-defeating approach to spirituality. Now he saw the path to noble living. This did not mean becoming a replica of the Buddha. His path was his own. By unifying his energies, he was able to live vibrantly. What is very striking to a reader of the Buddhist texts is that the Buddha's disciples were very varied personalities. The Buddha did not fit people into a mould. He gave them the courage to be true to reality. They all found ways to live wholesome, compassionate, positive lives, and they each did so in a manner which was distinctive and true to their different natures.

Part 2
Adversity

· 6 ·

Learning from Life

Many of the important things we learn the hard way. Looking back, I can see that the times of adversity have each taught me something which has given my life extra quality and depth, even though, at the time, I did not always welcome these challenges.

There was the time I lived in a monastery which was very poor. The diet was inadequate. The building was cold. Sometimes we would sit in meditation and snow would blow in under the eaves and settle gently upon our robes. On one occasion I was trapped in snow drifts overnight. On another, in the depths of the unusually hard winter, the water system froze for a week and we had to fetch all our water for washing and drinking in buckets across the snow from a spring. There was much hardship and I became seriously ill. People generally go to considerable lengths to avoid getting themselves into such situations. However, there is no doubt that I remember that time as one when I felt vibrantly alive. Many of the scenes live on in my memory for their exquisite beauty, the more vibrant for being associated with the emotions that accompany situations where one is near the limit of endurance. At the time, I would have preferred each of the details of the situation to have been otherwise, but through that experience I learnt to appreciate many things deeply that until then I had simply taken for granted.

Often what we learn from the experience of a less than comfortable life is compassion and kindness. I once lived in a fairly remote house on the moors. It was not an easy life and it was even harder for many of our neighbours who were hill farmers eking out a living from rocky fields in an adverse climate. People were, however, in general, more generous, friendly and willing to help one another than is common in the city.

When we experience obstacles and hardship, it can go either way with us. We may become bitter and alienated or we may grow as people. Experience broadens us. Difficult experiences challenge us. A person who has always lived in their own country, for instance, may not know what it is like to be a refugee or a member of an ethnic minority. A rich person has difficulty appreciating the concerns of the poor. The Buddha, who had been brought up rich, had to go to the other extreme, giving up everything, before he could really appreciate the wholeness of life. Akong Rimpoche, the Tibetan Buddhist teacher at the Kargyu Samye Ling community in Scotland, came to Britain as a refugee after the Chinese invasion of his country. He had been brought up to enjoy the prestige of an incarnate lama, a leader in the society of Tibet. He has spoken of how his experience working as a lavatory attendant when he first arrived in Britain as an exile taught him just as much, in a different way, as his monastic education had done: learning which has stood him in good stead in his subsequent work of compassion in the world. I think it is worth adding, however, that if he had not had the monastic education first, he might not have taken the experience of menial work so positively.

I believe that the Buddha's intention was to show us how to be enlightened rather than defeated by all the various situations of life. Affliction we will assuredly meet. He wanted us to meet it well.

Of course, the most difficult afflictions to bear are often psychological and social, rather than physical. It was a hardship to carry buckets of water across the snow, but it was also invigorating. It was, no doubt, unsavoury doing the work which Akong Rimpoche found himself doing, but the more trying part of this experience for most people would be the sense of humiliation and loss of accustomed role.

Some years ago I met with a series of setbacks which threw me into a state of depression. The black mood hung over me. There were many times when I would have preferred to be dead, not that I had any positive will to bring my life to an end. I must have been very difficult to live with at this time. Nonetheless, throughout all this period I retained a faith that, as I would put it, 'Nature must know what she is doing.' I did not try to economise on the experience of my gloomy feelings, nor did I exaggerate them. I was grateful that I had had some spiritual training to prepare me for eventualities of this kind. It is difficult to date the arrival and the lifting of such a mood. I endured between two and three years of gloom. Eventually my mental climate began to change, not a little assisted by the consistent support and tolerance of people who loved me. These events also changed me. A certain brashness and intolerance which I had when younger has given way. My previous assumption that 'I would never suffer from anything like that' has, perforce, been abandoned, and I am able to appreciate that there are many more hills and valleys in the landscape of life. I am now able to look back and regard the experience of depression as another precious milestone along my path.

The Buddha taught enlightenment. He did not teach that we will never be depressed. He taught us not to be defeated by it. He did not teach us how to avoid suffering. He taught us to meet affliction and live nobly, so that suffering is not unnecessarily multiplied. There is suffering enough in the world. He did not put himself above us. He was a man who never claimed divinity. He showed a way to live with reality, with all its alternations and with all the emotions and internal changes that result from them, and to see that this is our path.

When we consider the kinds of challenging experiences recorded in this chapter, we can see that whether they turn out to be victories or defeats for us in the end depend not upon the nature of the affliction itself so much as upon how we manage the emotions, thoughts, imaginings and impulses that arise in us at the time. As we manage our internal world, so shall our external life become.

Recognising adversity and affliction is a first step. Sometimes we fear to do so. A person coming into psychotherapy may have very little consciousness of what afflicts them. 'There are no problems in my family,' she says. 'I had a happy childhood.' Perhaps so, but there will also inevitably have been suffering and the blanket assertion that everything is all right may obscure examination of important factors shaping a person's life. It can preclude the learning of important lessons. Not infrequently, it is the client who asserts that all was and is well who turns out to have had the most troubled history. One of the first pieces of work I ever had to do as a social worker was to visit a family which was in complete disarray. As soon as I arrived, the mother announced quite vociferously: 'I don't know what you have come for. I am a perfect parent. There is nothing wrong here.' The assertion that problems do not exists may be a last ditch defence.

We all carry hurt within us. It is not possible to have gone through life without getting buffeted. The hurt we carry is fuel. It is one of the essential conditions for a fire. When a person, or a whole community, is spiritually impoverished, this fuel is stored up. It then becomes tinder dry. The potential for fire to get out of control is then great. This is when wars start. I asked an acquaintance from Sarajevo why he thought the civil war there broke out. He said: 'Boredom.' He meant that people's lives had ceased to be purposeful and war gave them a sense of direction. People sometimes fear that religion causes wars but, although religion, patriotism, self-interest, history and many other things may be invoked by war mongers, the real root of war is spiritual bankruptcy.

We are all carrying a lot of fuel. Fires can break out at any time. The client who comes to therapy typically says something like: 'I have such and such distress, but I do not know why.' Sometimes, after hearing just a little of what the person has been through or is currently enduring, one feels there is nothing pathological about their pain at all: it is simply the natural response to their situation. If a person believes that they should never have such feelings, however, they are likely to blame themselves or others. Wars, both internal and external, grow out of blame, and blame grows out of non-acceptance.

If a person does not recognise affliction then they are unlikely to set about doing anything constructive about it. Sometimes it may be thought that religion advocates a grin-and-bear-it stance in relation to troubles. Stoicism certainly has its place in building a strong character. We should not forget, however, that the Buddha's effect on many people was to lead them to give it all up and change their lifestyle radically. As a psychotherapist, I often feel some trepidation about bringing people face to face with the reality of their lives because, if they do so, the implications for necessary change may be major and one wonders whether the person will have the courage for it. Indeed, it may well often be because we have intuitive knowledge of what might be required of us that sometimes we prefer not to see. The Buddha hoped to inspire in us the spirit to tackle what needs to be done. When we have such spirit, we will not flinch from looking.

A Few Problems with the First Noble Truth

The First Noble Truth is the reality of affliction (*dukkha*). The Buddha set it out as follows. 'This is the Noble Truth about dukkha. Birth is dukkha. Ageing is dukkha. Sickness is dukkha. Death is dukkha. Sorrow, pain, grief and despair are dukkha. Association with what is unpleasant and separation from what is pleasant are dukkha. Not getting what one wants is dukkha. In short, the whole process of attachment is dukkha.' The First Noble Truth, therefore, is that dukkha is a fact of life.

Clearly the word dukkha means 'affliction'. The more common translation is 'suffering'. 'Suffering' is not wrong, but it does give the sense of something predominantly psychological whereas the list given in the Buddha's definition of dukkha includes such things as illness and death which are not predominantly psychological in the normal sense. In the normal usage of words, dukkha seems to consist primarily of unwelcome things that happen to us.

So what is the Buddha getting at by this statement? He calls it a Noble Truth. Why 'noble'? What can be noble about having unpleasant things happen to you? Most people find such events undignified and do everything they can to avoid them. Of course, this is a translation from the language in which the talk is written down and even that is not the language the Buddha himself actually spoke. There are, therefore, some hazards in us trying to construe what he must have meant. Let us begin by looking at the common interpretation.

The general view is this. The Noble Truth of suffering points out the problem. All people want to escape from suffering. The Second Truth points out the cause of suffering, which, we are told, is craving or desire or attachment. The Third Truth then becomes the way to overcome suffering which, logically, is by the extinction of desire. The Fourth Truth, marga, describes the path, the following of which leads us to the end of desire which in turn guarantees the ending of suffering. In this orthodox view, the Four Truths hold together as a logical set whose structure is as follows. X is the problem. X is caused by Y. Y can be eliminated. The way to eliminate it is Z. This is not the way that the Buddha sets out most of his other teachings. Many of his teachings are given in the form of logical propositions and they almost invariably have the linear form A leads to B which leads to C which leads to D and so on.

The fact that the Four Noble Truths do not follow this common pattern calls for an explanation. The traditional commentaries provide this by saying that this teaching is modelled on the way that a physician might speak about an illness. On this basis, the First Noble Truth tells us that the illness is suffering. Everywhere you look you see people burdened by suffering. It is an epidemic. The Second Noble Truth tells us that there is a cause for this illness. The cause is desire. Desire is the virus or germ which is responsible for this epidemic. The Third Noble Truth tells us that there is a cure which is destruction of desire. The Fourth Noble Truth sets out a treatment regime for the patient. If the patient follows these eight prescriptions, Right View, Right Thought and so on, they will be completely cured of the disease and will not be afflicted by suffering again.

This is the common interpretation found in a great many basic books on Buddhism. It is an interpretation that I have long felt to be unsatisfactory, but it took me many years to arrive at the alternative, given how well established this common interpretation is. In fact, one hesitates even to think that there might be an alternative. To make a substantial change in how we understand the Buddha's words in this most fundamental of his utterances is to move the foundation stone of a huge building which has been standing upon it for more than two millennia. Perhaps, therefore, this little book is unduly audacious. I am sure many will find it so. Nonetheless, I think that this is what is required, for reasons which I hope will become apparent.

The problems with the standard interpretation are several. The word translated as 'suffering' is dukkha. There has been a good deal of controversy about whether 'suffering' is, in fact, the right translation of this word and many alternatives such as 'unsatisfactoriness' or 'ill-being' have from time to time been offered, each of which has some merit. The point really is not what English word is best, but rather what did the Buddha really mean? Nonetheless, the reason for the controversy about the meaning of dukkha is revealing. This controversy occurs because many people, especially western people, have difficulty understanding what the Buddha is really saying when we are told in the standard interpretation, that dukkha is caused by desire. In order to make sense of his statement, there is an understandable temptation to think that the 'suffering' the Buddha is talking about is a mental phenomenon. Most of us can see fairly well how it could be that desire could make us suffer mentally. We do not see so readily how desire could make us get old, get physically ill, get born or die. Many western, and perhaps some eastern people, assume that the Buddha is talking only about mental suffering. That is not, however, what he says. Dukkha includes physical phenomena like illness and dying.

In the schools of Buddhism which are most strongly influenced by Indian culture, such as Tibetan and Theravada Buddhism, the traditional commentaries take it that the Buddha meant that mental phenomena in one lifetime give rise to physical phenomena in a subsequent life. In this view, we suffer physical birth, disease and death in this life because of desire, craving and attachment in previous lives. In the schools which evolved in the milieu of Chinese and central Asian civilization, this interpretation, while acknowledged, does not actually seem to be as firmly established in practice. As Buddhism comes to the west, resistance to its acceptance is even stronger.

It is not actually difficult to know what the Buddha meant by dukkha since the First Noble Truth is, among other things, a definition of the term. What is dukkha? Dukkha is birth, ageing, sickness, death, sorrow, pain, grief, despair, association with what is unpleasant, separation from what is pleasant, and not getting what one wants. All these are dukkha. Buddha's definition includes not just psychological elements, but also physical ones. In fact, most of what the Buddha includes in the definition of dukkha are things that happen to us. Although psychological factors undoubtedly play a part in our getting sick and dying at particular times and in particular ways, basically, these are things that happen to us. Similarly, 'not getting what we want' certainly has a psychological element since our mentality defines what we want but, basically, not getting what we want or need is something that happens to us.

You can understand from what I have just said, that my preference is to assume that the Buddha was talking in a fairly straightforward way which the ordinary person would have no difficulty understanding. I do not think that what he said was something you could only understand by being psychologically or metaphysically sophisticated. If it is possible to take what the Buddha says at face value, I would like to try doing so as the first line of approach. If that leaves us with something incomprehensible, then perhaps we need to look more deeply. That looking deeply, however, may be more a matter of re-examining our own preconceptions than twisting what the Buddha actually said.

This is important. If we construe the Four Noble Truths as saying that dukkha can be abolished, and we assume that the Buddha practised what he preached, then we are faced with the difficult question: Why did he get sick and die many years after his enlightenment? Can we say that he did not really mean that sickness and dying were dukkha? Did he use the terms sickness and dying metaphorically? Was he only referring to mental suffering? For a long time I, like many other people, was rather inclined to this interpretation, but really it does not hold water. The Buddha's definition of dukkha is very clear. Dying is dukkha and the Buddha died, so it is not correct to say that dukkha did not apply to the Buddha after his enlightenment. There was a time late in the Buddha's life when he got a thorn in his foot and the wound turned septic. The Buddha bore the pain with great fortitude. It is not true that he did not suffer pain. Enlightenment did not make him immune to stepping on a thorn, nor to the ensuing pain. Dukkha did not and does not cease with enlightenment.

Another problem with the usual interpretation is the implication it has for relationships. Many people when they hear the Buddhist teaching for the first time, quite understandably say:

Does that mean that when your husband, wife or mother dies, you should not grieve? If the secret of happiness is to give up attachment, does that mean that one should not love anyone? Many Buddhists do take the teaching as having an implication of this kind. The life of the monk or nun is held up as the ideal and this is said to be one in which all attachments to particular people have been abolished. The monk or nun is therefore believed to be closer to the state in which dukkha cannot arise. For many people, however, this idea seems suspect. Grief is a natural healthy process. The Buddha suffered some very grievous losses. The execution of his patron, King Bimbisara, must have been a terrible blow. Everyday, the Buddha met people who told him about their various sufferings. He will have felt for them. The Buddha left the family life, we are told, but the fact is that most of his close relatives took to the road with him. He was accompanied by his son, his wife, his aunt, and several of his cousins. Many of these people remained his close companions throughout his life. The notion that his path was one of rejecting close relationships does not seem to hold up.

Furthermore, this idea has a pernicious effect. It can make us ashamed to suffer. If we believe that the goal of Buddhism is to eliminate suffering from our lives and that, in the form of the Eightfold Path, we have the means to do so, then our personal suffering is a mark of our failure. Are advanced practitioners allowed to have personal problems? As Buddhism is absorbed into western culture, there is growing unease among many long-experienced practitioners about the fact that, even after many years of meditative practice, they still experience the whole range of emotions, confusion, suffering and grief that are associated with the conduct of personal relationships in a world of impermanence. This unease is one of the driving forces behind the concern of many people, myself included, to achieve some kind of integration of Buddhism with psychotherapy, the latter being unashamedly directed toward helping people come to terms with their personal emotions. For many, therefore, this concern is directed to repairing what seems like the failure of traditional Buddhist practice to address this real human need. My suggestion in this book is that this arises from misunderstanding what the Buddha actually taught.

· 8 ·

Noble and True

If the common interpretation of the First Noble Truth does not hold up, what was the Buddha really getting at? If he was not saying that we should abolish attachment and so make ourselves immune to suffering, what was the real point of his teaching?

The Buddha called these four points Noble Truths. He might have chosen this term simply to emphasise their importance and, I think, this is how most people take this title. I suspect, however, that something more precise was intended. The talk on setting the Dharma wheel in motion is very succinct. Not a word is wasted. The Buddha had been thinking hard for several weeks about how to get the essence of his message across to his former friends who, he knew, would initially be disinclined to accept it. He wanted to make every word count. To people who see the Buddha's teaching already well established and the Buddha covered with prestige, it is natural enough to think that he can glorify his teachings by calling them noble and true. We must, however, allow for the fact that this was not the situation at the time when this talk was given. At that time the Buddha was an unknown young teacher who had just walked out of the forest. I therefore believe that the term Noble Truth was descriptive and informative in a more precise and a more straightforward sense.

True means real. When the Buddha says that affliction is a truth, he means that it is real. When he defines it, the examples he gives are things which are very real, like sickness and death. These are inescapable realities. When the Buddha says that affliction is a truth, I do not think that he is saying that it is something which can be escaped. Quite the contrary. He is pointing out that it cannot be escaped. Dukkha is inescapable.

To suffer affliction is authentic. It is real and it makes life real. The point being made here is not that we cannot escape from particular afflictions. Clearly we can. If hungry, we can eat; if cold, wrap up; and so on. But we cannot create a life in which affliction will not occur. A life in which there was no affliction would be flaccid and unreal. To set up such a meaningless existence as the goal would be folly. The Buddha did not teach escape from affliction. A life completely free from affliction, such as his father had tried to contrive for him, is not authentic. The Buddha, therefore, taught that suffering will always be part of our lives as long as we live. After enlightenment we see and feel this more clearly, not less. This is the direct opposite of what is generally taught in Buddhist textbooks where enlightenment is conceptualised as an escape. In making this statement Buddha is recapitulating his own experience over many painful years. He is saying, 'I have tried to escape from suffering by every means known to man. I have tested all the prescriptions to their very limits and have found them wanting. There is no escape from affliction.'

So much for the word 'truth' What about the word 'noble'? This word is, I suggest, even more important. Noble means worthy of respect. Something respectable is something which we do not need to feel ashamed about. The basic reason that we try to escape from suffering is not the simple fact that suffering hurts. People often bear things that hurt and may even choose to go into situations where they know they will be hurt. A soldier goes into battle expecting, at the very least, to have an arduous time ahead and knowing the risk of mutilation and death. This example is not distant from the Buddha's experience, since he was himself brought up to be a warrior. He knew that the worthy soldier faces hardship and danger out of a sense of nobility, and noble is the word he chose in this first talk.

Noble also means courageous. Calling suffering a noble thing does not at all suggest that it is something to be avoided or escaped from. The Buddha is saying that to be a human being who necessarily suffers is a dignified thing to be. What he is overthrowing is the idea that the spiritual quest consists of a flight from suffering. On the contrary, it is the flight which is undignified and shameful. Confronting and overcoming problems may seem like a painful process and most may seek to avoid it, but such avoidance simply leads to greater pain and indignity.

It is undignified to indulge oneself to excess. It is undignified to get drunk. It is undignified to be involved in illicit sexual acts. It is undignified to hop from one entertainment to the next. It is undignified to be dominated by the pursuit of money and comfort. It is undignified to tell untruths in order to impress people. All these forms of indulgence are ignoble

But it is also undignified to starve yourself until your ribs stick out, to go about naked in the cold, to plead with heaven, to kill animals supposedly to please the gods, to hold your breath until you pass out, or to mutilate your body with thongs and thorns. Practices which are supposedly spiritual, but which are really motivated by a desire to achieve immunity from suffering or to get special treatment from the fates, are not really respectable. It is a supreme irony that Buddhism has come to be characterised as a path for those who wish to escape from suffering.

What the Buddha understood and what he makes clear in the First Noble Truth is that pride and dignity play a central role in human psychology. If I may make a play upon Freudian language the 'nobility principle' is far more powerful than either the 'pleasure principle' or the 'reality principle' in determining human actions. Buddha taught a noble path – or, we could say, a sublime path. To suffer the suffering which is inherent in our being, without resort to a strategy of undignified flight, whether by worldly or supposedly spiritual means, is real nobility.

We know that the nobility principle goes beyond the reality principle since, in the service of nobility, people will readily attempt the impossible. The interesting thing is that it is often by attempting the impossible in good spirit that the greatest things are achieved. The Zen Master Shunryu Suzuki is famous for the remark: 'To think, "Because it is possible we will do it," is not Buddhism. Even though it is impossible, we have to do it because our true nature wants us to.' Martin Luther King set out to bring complete equality into relations between black and white people. Gandhi set out to bring peace, harmony and self-determination to his country. If they had considered the likelihood of success realistically they might never have begun.

Calling affliction a Noble Truth is liberating because pride and dignity play such a central part in human psychology. When we look deeply into ourselves, we are likely to find that, at some deep level, we are ashamed of our infirmities. In the media we are constantly assailed by images of health and beauty. Insofar as we are not like that we feel ashamed. There is a sense in which the word dukkha might be translated as 'imperfection'. The Buddha is saying that there is no shame in being imperfect. Again, this is quite different from what many people think religion, Buddhism included, is about.

Ideally, we would not die, would not grow old, would not get sick, would not ever have to associate with unpleasant things and would always be surrounded by the pleasant, the beautiful and the comfortable. Our teeth would not come out, our eyesight would not fail, our skin would not wrinkle, our hair would not turn grey. This is the vision of heaven, and religions are as apt to trade on it as are the advertising agents of consumerism. Our lives do not conform to this heavenly picture so we feel a corresponding shame. Then we either spend huge amounts of money hiding the fact that we are not perfect specimens and distracting ourselves from the unpleasant aspects of our lives, or we wear ourselves out in supposedly spiritual procedures that enable us to believe that we are, or are on the way to becoming, members of the chosen few who will live in heaven. We put on a front for the world and cover up our infirmities because we are ashamed. The Buddha, however, taught that it is better to live in the human world than in heaven. Buddhism is not a quest for heaven. This fact alone marks it out as different from other spiritual paths.

The Buddha's teaching starts with an assault upon the shame we feel about our suffering. He says that dukkha – imperfection, suffering – is real and we do not need to be ashamed of it. In fact, facing inevitable affliction is noble. A noble person is one who accepts the reality of adversity and is not investing energy either in avoiding the necessity to deal with it or in exacerbating it. The salvation of humankind will be found in the practice of a noble response to existential reality. That is enlightenment.

Nirvana is Birth and Death

The First Noble Truth on its own is capable of revolutionising our lives. It is not just preliminary to what follows. The other three Noble Truths which we shall come to are also very powerful medicine but, in a way, they are elaborations. The vital first principle is this first assertion that dukkha is real and respectable. If we can begin to see that all the things grouped under the term dukkha are respectable realities and therefore are the building blocks of a noble life, this itself constitutes a great liberation. It means that we can begin now. We do not have to wait for different circumstances, outer or inner. I meet many people who are still in the waiting room of life. This teaching enables us to start living fully, wherever we may be.

Many centuries after the Buddha, the Japanese Zen Master Dogen (1200–52) wrote about the First Noble Truth in the following words: 'The most important issue for Buddhists is how to get a completely clear appreciation of birth and death. Buddha (i.e. enlightenment) exists within birth and death. So birth and death (as a problem) vanish. Birth and death (as reality) are nirvana. If you see this you will not seek nirvana by trying to avoid birth and death. This is the way to be free from birth and death. This is the most important point in Buddhism.' This passage appears as the first paragraph of a text called *Shushogi*. The *Shushogi* was compiled after Dogen's death to bring together in just a few pages the distilled essence of his teaching. Just like the teaching of the Buddha himself, it begins with this elucidation of the First Noble Truth.

The word 'shushogi' indicates 'the meaning of enlightened practice'. The title is significant because a theme running through the whole of Dogen's writings is the identity of practice and enlightenment. Again and again he teaches that one does not practise *in order to reach* enlightenment: practice is enlightenment and enlightenment is practice. Where Dogen writes 'birth and death' the Buddha said 'dukkha'. We could, therefore, rewrite Dogen's statement as follows: 'The important point is to see dukkha as it is. Enlightenment is within dukkha. Dukkha is not a problem. Dukkha is nirvana. To search for nirvana outside of dukkha is just foolish. Understand this and you are free.' A very clear statement indeed.

The truly noble life, therefore, is to live one's life just as it really is. All the aspects of it that one has been in flight from are actually the very things that make life noble. This is much easier to see in others than in ourselves! When we see a person who accepts adversity or trouble and goes on living in a positive way without resorting to escapism we cannot help feeling inspired. In our own case however, we can very easily succumb to self-pity.

Dukkha, as such, is not a problem. Problems only exist in relation to some purpose that we have. Lack of food might be a problem for many people, but would not be a problem for somebody who was on hunger strike, for instance. Lack of money is only a problem in relation to a desire to buy something, and so on. So, in order to see whether dukkha is a problem or not, we have to look at the purpose of life. In the modern world, the purpose for many has become to feel pleasure all the time. Such a purpose is completely self-defeating, since it makes most of what happens in life into a problem. Then we feel stressed.

Dogen and the Buddha both accept that if one's purpose is to live a life devoted to pleasure, comfort and worldly advancement, then dukkha is a big obstacle. They also accept that many people who have not looked deeply into the matter may well think that this is indeed what life is about. What they are pointing out, however, is that this is a shallow view. Really, people are not fundamentally motivated by pleasure alone. There are things that are more important to all of us than pleasure. Fundamentally we want to live lives that we can feel good about. We accumulate wealth, status, power and pleasures as means to this end, as we believe, but when life pushes us to an extremity, our bluff is called.

Often enough a person, like Peter in chapter two, may do all the things that society suggests will lead to satisfaction, only to feel disappointed and cheated. The Buddha had a head start in this respect, since he was provided with all the conventional 'goods' from a young age and was able to discover early in life that they do not satisfy the most basic human motivation. This most basic motivation is to live a life that one can respect oneself for living, a life that is noble. Noble is a rather old-fashioned word and there is no word that I can think of in common modern usage that provides a more satisfactory translation of the word *aryan* that the Buddha used to describe this fundamental human motivation. Perhaps this is a sign of how far removed modern life has become from basic human needs. We do, however, talk about 'human dignity' and this is close to what the Buddha is getting at.

Enlightenment means to experience with complete clarity the fact that dukkha – the travail of being born, working, relating to others, growing up, growing old and so on – is part and parcel of human dignity; that all attempts to run away from it are undignified and that this applies just as much to spiritually, psychologically or socially sophisticated forms of escapism as it does to worldly or primitive ones. People are not made happy by an endless supply of pleasures. Many rich people are miserable. People are happy when they live noble lives. Misery is not created by lack of pleasure, but by resentment, bitterness, and the degradation of character. Rich people do not generally accumulate their wealth in order to have pleasures. They accumulate wealth because they think this will make them respectable. In this way they hope to set their minds at rest. Of course, in reality quite the opposite often results. The means by which wealth is accumulated often involves action which leaves a stain of guilt that the person never manages to live down.

There is a great difference between appearances and reality. The desire to achieve the appearance of nobility often destroys the substance of nobility. The most noble thing that young Siddhartha saw in his early life was not the wealth and pageantry that surrounded his illustrious family, but the gait of a passing holy man who walked through the town square unaffected by the hustle and bustle. Appearance without substance is unauthentic. This *saddhu* was noble precisely because he was not ruffled by concerns about keeping up appearances, nor by anxieties about the ups and downs of circumstance. He was noble in his chosen poverty.

By making the respectable reality of dukkha into the first point of his teaching, the Buddha is not saying that all life is suffering. He is saying that life is everything life is. It includes birth *and* death, health *and* disease, youth *and* ageing, pleasure *and* pain, success *and* failure, meeting *and* parting. A life that we can be happy to live is not one in which we are constantly trying to have one half of each of these pairings without having the other half. Birth implies death. Health implies disease. Youth implies ageing. Pleasure implies pain. Success implies failure. Meeting implies parting. You cannot have one without the other and to try to live as if you could leads to all kinds of unnecessary trouble. Dukkha is half of life and it has just as much dignity as the other half. Night is as dignified as day.

Dukkha is no impediment to true happiness. The idea that Buddhism leads to happiness is correct. The idea that it does so by eliminating dukkha is false. The First Noble Truth points to the possibility of happiness within dukkha, and dukkha within happiness. The two go together. We will grow old and die and we can be happy. The one does not preclude the other. We can die happy.

It is unwise to wish for the end of all problems. Actually, a person who is functioning healthily in a psychological sense has many more problems than the person on the back ward of a psychiatric institution. What problems does such an inmate have? Their needs are all provided for and there is nothing to do. If you want no more problems, just go insane. There are no problems in a meaningless life. No, a sane life is one problem after another. Everyday we solve a vast number of little and some big problems. That is how we gain satisfaction and it is how our lives are brought to some maturity.

Kyong Ho, (1849–1912) was a famous Korean Zen Master. He taught: 'Don't ask for perfect health – that's just greed: make medicine from the suffering in sickness. Don't hope to be without problems – that's just laziness: accept life's difficulties. Don't expect your path to be free from obstacles – without them the fire of your enlightenment will go out: find liberation within the disturbances themselves.'

If there were no suffering in the world, consciousness would never have evolved in the first place Without consciousness the possibility of bliss would not arise. Those who want to return to the kind of nirvana which is just an inanimate state are completely missing the point of the Buddha's teaching. As Buddhists we may bow before statues, but this is not because we want to be statues. It is all right for the statue to be a statue, but a person is a person. Statues do not become enlightened and do not experience love, compassion, joy and bliss.

Kondañña suddenly realized how all the effort he had put into ascetic practice had been intended to get him to a point where he would be immune. He saw the great irony that our very effort to avoid the normal and natural elements of adversity creates far more suffering than the original affliction itself. He felt a great joy in his heart as he saw what he had to do. There is happiness in knowing for sure what we must do. What was necessary was to live a noble life. If he did that his heart would always be at peace. That is nirvana.

Part 3

Passion

Freedom to Feel

The First Noble Truth is concerned with what happens to us. The Second Noble Truth is about the feelings that arise in us in response. The essential meaning of both these two Truths is that there is no cause for shame in either of these domains. These two Truths together constitute a charter of freedom for the human spirit.

If birth and death are nirvana, then the passions that birth and death generate are the stuff of awakening. You need a lot of clay to make a big buddha, said Dogen,[1] and he was not just talking about statues. It is a fundamental principle of Buddhism that only sentient beings get enlightened. It is our clay feet, our essential humanity, our very imperfection, that ensures that we have the potential to generate the necessary passion. The error that many have made is to think that after enlightenment sentience, the capacity for normal feelings, has somehow ceased.

The Second Noble Truth is *samudaya*. The second half of this word, *-udaya*, means 'to go up'. It derives from the word *ut* meaning 'up'. The first part of the word, *sam*, means 'with' or 'together'. Combining these we get 'co-arising' or 'coming up along with'. Hence 'response'. *Dukkha samudaya*, which is the name the Buddha gives to the Second Noble Truth, thus means 'response to dukkha'. In the Second Truth, therefore, the Buddha says that something co-arises with dukkha. With dukkha there is a response in us. That is what sentience means: we respond.[2]

What is it that co-arises with dukkha? A longing for things to be otherwise. Fight and flight. The Buddha calls it 'thirst' (*trishna*). Often this word 'thirst' is translated as 'craving' which conveys the sense quite well, though for reasons which we will come to it is important not to lose track of the fact that the word the Buddha actually used was 'thirst'. Loosely, this term refers to most of what we call feelings or passions. We can see that the Buddha was speaking in the ordinary language of his day. With the first two Truths he is saying: life inevitably involves affliction and we inevitably have feelings when this happens. This state of affairs is noble: it is OK. There is nothing wrong with us that we have feelings when we are afflicted. He does not say that he himself no longer has such feelings.

I think it is very important to clarify the meaning here since there is a common idea that Buddhism implies elimination of feelings. Not at all. The Second Noble Truth tells us that feelings are facts and as such they are completely natural and acceptable. Problems do not arise from the fact of having feelings. Problems arise from what we do with them or from our attempts to avoid having them.

When we are troubled we long for our state of affairs to change. Or, to put the same thing another way, we long to re-create ourselves. We unrealistically long for a trouble-free existence. We would like our lives to be free of dukkha. That would be heaven. The urge to be rid of what afflicts us is the thirst or craving that the Buddha is referring to. In the moment of experiencing dukkha, we also experience an urge to remake our life in some way which will be free from this trouble. This 'remaking our life' (or craving for rebirth) may be a very small thing or a very large thing. If the dukkha is that my body is feeling cold, the urge to recompose myself may take the form of a desire to move a little closer to the fireplace. If the dukkha is that all the people who have ever loved me have been wiped out by a terrible war which has ravaged my country, then the urge to recompose myself may take the form of a rage for vengeance or, more properly, for the destruction of the destroyers in a vain attempt to put the clock back. If the dukkha is that my stomach is empty, the urge may be to eat. If the dukkha is that I have been humiliated and my life's work has been held up to ridicule, the urge may be to commit suicide and so escape from this world altogether. We can see that some cravings suggest sensible actions and others do not.

The thirst or craving that the Buddha describes is the natural urge to escape from affliction and he is pointing out that this is an attempt to remake our life into a new form which will be suffering-free. Such an urge arises quite naturally. Really, it arises independently of our control. We have no say in its arising. In terms of our subjective experience, therefore, it is outside of what we experience as 'self'. As we saw in the last chapter, dukkha is something that happens to us. Samudaya is also something that happens to us. By training ourselves we may change the content and form of our response to a given stimulus, but respond we will.

The Buddha calls this response-ability a Noble Truth in just the same way as he called affliction noble and true. To say that 'co-arising' is noble is to say that there is nothing to be ashamed of in this first arising of craving. It is quite natural that when the bitter side manifests, we feel an immediate impulse to pull away from it. The reaction of pulling away from pain is an essential instinct without which it would be very hard for us to survive as individuals or as a species. If this impulse were not part of our natural functioning, life would be dangerous and much more difficult than it is. So it is natural and not ignoble that this urge arises.

Consciousness probably evolved in order to enable living beings to avoid harm. The circumstance in which we exist is one in which there is risk. If there was no risk of harm around us, there would never have been such a thing as consciousness. Consciousness[3] consists of the impulses that arise in circumstances of uncertainty. The important thing that the Buddha is saying is that we should not be ashamed of what we are. We do not need to be ashamed of the fact that thirst or craving arise. I think this is why the Buddha chose the word 'thirst' rather than 'craving'. Thirst is natural. Nobody needs to be ashamed of being thirsty. In the same way, nobody need be ashamed of having feelings.

Although feelings are not shameful, they do present problems. We long to be free of the affliction but sometimes it is not immediately removable and, even if it is, it may well return. When we grieve, we long for the return of the person we have lost. It does not happen, however strong our longing. When we are dry, we may drink and quench our thirst. We cannot, however, prevent it returning. There is a measure of unavoidable pain. Unfortunately, our efforts to avoid the inevitable often multiply our troubles. The Buddha was concerned to help us avoid piling unnecessary suffering on top of the unavoidable.

GRIEF

Much of what is called dukkha is covered by the English word 'loss'. We can see from what we know of the Buddha's own life that loss and grief were what concerned him. Loss is an affliction that cannot be undone. He could not bring his mother back. Loss is dukkha. When we suffer loss, we experience much pain. Grief can be very physical. When our world is turned upside down by the loss of somebody close to us, the adjustment we have to make is a great challenge to our spirit. Grief is a period of swinging from one extremity of mood to another in the wake of a serious disruption in our lives. Many books have been written on the subject of the 'grief reaction'.[4] A person in the grip of grief knows very well that these feelings are not under their control. Loss is dukkha. Grief is samudaya. It arises on the back of affliction and we can do nothing to stop it without seriously psychologically or physically damaging ourselves.

Grief is not just something that happens when somebody close to us dies. It is also the normal reaction to any major life change.[5] The person who is of strong spirit goes through this pain and emerges more mature and more compassionate. Frequently, however, a person will avoid doing this 'grief work', with unfortunate consequences which are well documented by western psychology.

Grief is like a fire burning within us. When a fire is started by a spark all the energy that has been stored up in the sticks over a long time past is released together as fire. When somebody dies, it is not just the event of death, but all the energy that has accumulated over a long relationship that is released as grief. Our response to affliction is commonly out of all proportion to the event itself because it releases what has been stored up in us over a long time. When such a fire is upon us, it feels as compelling as a raging thirst. At the time it is not easy to believe that the passion will pass. The Buddha warns us that this is a dangerous time. This is the time when we may do something rash which will bring much more trouble to ourselves and to those around us. In another talk on the same subject he gives a very drastic example. He says that lepers sometimes experience terrible itching. There is nothing they can do to prevent the itching arising. The itching is dukkha. When the itching comes, the craving to be free from it is so powerful that sometimes you may see a leper put his arm into a fire because, for a short time, the sensation of having your flesh burned away is actually less bad than the itching. Thus, in order to escape from one suffering, the leper inflicts something far more terrible upon himself, something which will cause him suffering for many years to follow.

This image of the leper putting his arm into the fire is a parable of our own lives. We may not be lepers, but we are all afflicted in some way. Along with the dukkha, up will come the craving: the itch. In the grip of this craving we may easily act in ways that are like getting seriously burned.

Passion does not have to be destructive like that. The fire of grief can be a cleansing fire that leaves us more pure and more mature, just as ore is smelted into metal. The Buddha dreamt of his mother. He grieved for her. This was something he could never shake off. His desire to indulge himself in the palace and then his desire to punish himself through ascetic practices can all be seen as arising from this central grief which would not go away. These two strategies were a bit like the leper. He was trying to cut off the trouble. Passion may also, however, inspire and sustain us.

There is a passage in the story of the Buddha to which is paid little attention by western readers. This is the occasion when the Buddha visits his mother in heaven[6] It is in this passage that we learn how the Buddha thought constantly about his mother and longed to see her, which is very understandable if we allow that buddhas have feelings. He goes to repay his debt of gratitude to her and does so by teaching her the Dharma. He is the fruit of her womb. The Dharma is the fruit of his life.

As he speaks, milk begins to flow from her breasts. It streams down and enters his mouth. She then says that she has never known such happiness before. It is as though a person suffering the pangs of severe hunger were to be given delicious food. She goes toward the Buddha, floating through the air. When the Buddha sees her he is overjoyed. He again teaches her the Dharma, saying: 'Until now you have swung between pleasure and pain. From now on please practise the noble path of enlightenment.' Queen Maya then speaks a verse of praise, says that his debt of gratitude will be repaid by cutting off the root of her greed, hate and delusion, and affirms her complete faith in him.

I have come to believe that the relationship with his dead mother was the driving force in the life of the Buddha. This vision of his visit to her in heaven would be entirely to be expected. It was his sense of his debt of gratitude to her that gave him the energy to go to such lengths in the quest for enlightenment and then to continue so tirelessly in his ministry to the world. The Buddha knew all about the way that we carry affliction within us. This pain of separation from his mother was a great passion. It was also a great driving force: a cleansing force. If he had not had this dukkha, he would not have become a great being. He saw clearly that dukkha is a fire and fire can burn and destroy, or it can be the power source that we need. We need that kind of fire to live a noble life.

Again and again in psychotherapy we see the deep need people have to be reconciled with their parents. The Buddha, after his enlightenment and the establishment of his teaching, went home and resolved the differences that existed between his father and himself. His dead mother remained harder to reach. Eventually, his work upon himself culminated in this visionary encounter with her in which he experiences a great catharsis. He is able to offer the fruit of his life's work to her and she is able to nourish him as she had been unable to do physically. In this psychodrama, the Buddha works through the central and deepest trauma of his life. This happens well after his enlightenment. We should not think that an awakened being is without personal issues to resolve. An awakened being is one whose enlightenment is constantly unfolding. The processes of therapy are not just for those who are failing. They are also appropriate to those on the highest path.

We live on a very beautiful planet. Many lovely things are to be found here. There are cherry trees and oak trees. There are birds that sing. There is sunshine and rain. There are mangoes and pomegranates, apples and oranges. The ocean around us is a constantly changing miracle. In this beautiful place we have been born as human beings, the most talented of all the wonderful creatures that inhabit this world. We are capable of love and understanding and happiness. In fact, the basic condition in which we exist is heavenly. Yet all this happiness seems so fragile. So easily, it seems, it can all be swept away or broken by events that are beyond our control. A stone can fall into the beautiful pond of our life and its mirror-like surface is suddenly convulsed and opaque. At such times we are liable to lose touch with our happiness. Then we forget that the pond has the capacity to swallow the stone and to return to its original beautiful state. We fail to foresee that when the stone has settled it may well prove to be an enhancement to the beauty of our lake. All the troubles that arise have the potential to be experiences of learning and growth from which we may emerge stronger and richer, but we do not always remember this at the time.

We think that the stone landing in our pond is the reason for our unhappiness. The Buddha points out, however, that the real trouble is that we perpetuate the disturbance ourselves by the way we either deny or overemphasise our natural response to it. We cannot avoid natural disturbances happening. We cannot help responding. But we do not have to let this response play havoc with our lives. The unrealistic attempt to extinguish affliction permanently, just like the leper who extinguishes the itch by burning the arm, does great damage. The acceptance of the noble reality of our passion, however, can be a great cleansing: a catharsis that helps us to make something of our life.

Asking for Help

Running away from trouble, we are failures. This constant failure is a source of shame. This shame goes deep, a self-incapacitating backdrop to our lives far worse in its effects than the hardships we are trying to escape from. It was to provide an antidote to this self-defeat that the Buddha introduced the term 'noble'. He constantly talked about what he offered people as 'the noble way'. He was saying that there is a cure for this shame. There is no way of escaping from changeableness – that is part and parcel of life – but there is no need to be ashamed: no need to pile inner torment on top of outer affliction by self-blame and inadequacy.

Because we are failures in our endless attempts to eliminate dukkha, we adopt dysfunctional strategies. We hide our feelings and fear to give ourselves away by asking for help. People go about their lives in denial, pretending all is well. We keep up a front. Other people all seem to be all right. Only we ourselves seem to have troubles. So we pretend to be all right too and feel fraudulent. 'Other people think I am strong and that I have got my life together, but I know that inside I am weak and a mess.' This, or something very like it, is the secret conviction of millions of people. The reason that other people all seem to be all right is that they are pretending, too.

Dukkha, in very basic ways, affects everybody. Everybody is affected by hunger, for instance. In modern life we have understandably tried to create a society in which famine never arises. Many modern people cannot conceive what it would be like to go without food for a day or two. However, in insulating ourselves from want, we have impoverished ourselves in a much more profound sense. We have lost our spirit.

The human spirit depends upon the stimulation provided by a degree of adversity. Before modern times famine was common. Even today, it is not possible to live as a human being without experiencing discomforts associated with eating and digesting. Over-eating also creates problems. Every day nature prompts us to eat. We can fast for a week or even two or three, but we can never become independent of this neediness. We depend upon getting food.

The Buddha taught his disciples this lesson in a very concrete way. Every day they went out to beg. With their bowl they stood in front of one house after another. It was their practice to make no discrimination between houses which were known to be generous and ones which were not. At each house the monk or nun had the experience of waiting to see if anything would be put in the bowl. If nothing was put in the bowl, they went hungry. An empty bowl is dukkha. This practice of begging is a powerful experiential lesson.

Most of us feel too ashamed to beg and this does not just relate to food. We experience a great range of uncomfortable emotions when we need to ask for something. 'I don't need anybody's help,' we assert defiantly. To ask for help is to admit that there is dukkha in our own lives, too. It provokes that sense of being a failure again. Many people would rather suffer than face their embarrassment. A person who comes into psychotherapy, for instance, may have taken the most courageous step when they finally admitted that they need help.

The Buddha, however, taught us that there is nothing shameful in begging for what is genuinely needed. He taught that to do so is a supremely important practice. Begging was not simply an expedient means for getting the monks and nuns fed. This could be readily achieved without the alms round. The practice was designed to bring home the basic facts of life and to help overcome the shame associated with making needs known. The monk or nun standing in dignified calm with her or his empty bowl is the embodiment of the Noble Truths.

Of course, even more imperious than hunger is thirst. We cannot go long without liquid. The word the Buddha chose was thirst. Anybody who thinks that the Buddha was talking about permanently bringing what the Second Noble Truth points out to an end is, in effect, saying that an enlightened person would no longer experience thirst. I think the Buddha chose this word, in the hot climate of India, to bring home to his listeners precisely the fact that this is not something that can be abolished.

However enlightened we may become we will still experience thirst. He is saying that it is such an intrinsic part of life that we should have no shame concerning it. Every day he got hungry and thirsty. Every day he took up his bowl and went into the nearest village and begged from house to house. This was the daily enactment of the teaching he gave. Dukkha is real. Thirst is real. It is real for the enlightened and the unenlightened alike. The enlightened are no longer ashamed of it and so do not live their lives in flight and pretence. Thus they are able to live a much more straight-forward, honest existence.

The Buddha taught his disciples to beg so that they learned not to be ashamed of need. He also taught them to fast for half the day so that they learned how to live in a way that was not dictated by appetite. It is noble to acknowledge the reality of need in a dignified way, without either exaggeration or denial. Need is discipline, not punishment.

The essence of our interpretation, then, of the Second Noble Truth is that it indicates that feelings are natural, inevitable and not something to be ashamed of. They are real and they are noble. Samudaya, 'that which comes up with affliction', is something which happens to us. To be responsive and have feelings avoids the extremes. One extreme is to deny, repress or feel ashamed. The other extreme is to allow our feelings to be the sole voice running our life and to fall into self-indulgent behaviour governed by whim. The former piles unnecessary suffering on top of unavoidable discomfiture. The latter renders us erratic and characterless.

Affliction is loss. Loss brings grief. Grief is not shameful. Grief is samudaya. Every day there are many little griefs and, from time to time, we suffer a major loss which reminds us in the most penetrating way of the truth of our existential situation: everything changes; nothing is substantial; and anything can be a cause of grief. The noble person has the capacity to live vibrantly in a world which is intrinsically both wonderful and terrible. This is not achieved by repressing feelings, nor by being ruled by them, but by accepting them, valuing them and wisely containing them. Such is the making of character.

Human relationships will be brought onto a much more satisfactory footing if we can understand and accept our response-ability and our need. There are times when we may honestly say 'I am suffering; please help,' just as there are times when it is appropriate to say, 'I see that you are suffering; I am here.' So often, in the revelation of people's lives that comes through psychotherapy, we find that a person has got stuck in one position. They are either cast as the dependent victim or as the self reliant strong one who has no needs. These two positions are fictions. To give help and to receive it are both noble and natural. The Buddha pointed out the way to return human relations to a healthy honesty in which giving and receiving accord with the realities of our ever fluctuating circumstances. In the acts of giving and receiving, simply performed and naturally accepted, without melodrama, the spiritual path is enacted. As children we learn to say 'please' and 'thank you' and these basic gestures are the building blocks from which mature and intimate human relations develop. The idea that an enlightened person is one without needs and feelings is one of the most dangerous of all the pitfalls that lie scattered along the spiritual path.

A person may not recognise their fire, may not become conscious of the feelings that come up in them. Although we may recognise what afflicts us, we may lie to ourselves about our own reactions, or our self-image may be so strong that part of what is happening to us never comes to consciousness. Many western therapies, both humanistic and analytic, try to address this area. A greater sensitivity to samudaya, to what is arising, is a likely outcome from psychotherapeutic work in many different approaches. Buddhism places huge stress upon the importance of awareness.

People fear fire. We fear our feelings. We fear their potential for destructive effect. Many people go through life trying to protect others from their feelings. They have never learned how to handle them safely and do not want to get burned. The commonest reason for unassertive behaviour is suppressed anger. The person is not assertive because they fear that if they start to be so a great torrent of invective may escape and cause untold harm. Despite what we know is inside us, we want to stay calm. It is a kind of kindness to others, but there is a better way. The better way is to train our character so that we have the fire and we have it under control. Then we will act in the way that people call confident.

This requires self-control. The wind that can whip the fire into a destructive inferno is the wind of greed, hate and delusion. In Buddhist terms, these are collectively referred to as 'ego'. This Buddhist use of the term 'ego' is quite close to common usage. It can, however, cause a bit of confusion since most western systems of psychotherapy do not use the word 'ego' in the common way. Freudian, Jungian and other systems each have their own technical definitions of the term which are often far removed from the way it is used in common speech. Buddhism sees ego as something that gets in the way of natural, healthy psychological functioning. In Buddhism, strength of character corresponds to absence of ego.

Ego is a fixed sense of self. By holding onto a particular self concept, we close our minds to at least some of the feelings that are constantly bubbling up and some of the information provided by the impact of external reality. We get into what the Buddha called 'not seeing'[1] Essentially this is an attempt to stay in control in a way that closes part of us down. Its effect however is simply to keep the painful parts of our life out of view and, consequently, out of our control. When Jesus said, 'Get thee behind me, Satan,' he may not have been being very wise. When Satan is behind us, we cannot see what he is up to. It is better to have him somewhere where we can keep an eye on him.

Often enough a client presents themselves to a psychotherapist saying that they are out of touch with their feelings. What we see from the first two Noble Truths is that feelings arise from exposure to particular stimuli. A person who is out of touch with their feelings is probably not facing their affliction either. What comes up in us is largely a series of conditioned responses. For a person to find their feelings, it is not generally a matter of looking for feelings. It is more commonly a matter of holding the person's attention on the stimulus that may be expected to produce them. A person with a delayed grief reaction, for instance, will not progress by talking about grief. They will start to grieve when they face the reality that 'Jack is dead'. It may often be the role of the therapist to re-present to them the hard reality.

There are also some people, ones who are quite likely to be diagnosed as mentally ill, who have reached the point where they no longer recognise what a healthy emotion is. A person recovering from schizophrenia, for instance, may well interpret any arising of feelings as a sign that they are relapsing into madness. People who hear voices frequently only have this symptom when their feelings are absent. People who suffer from mania are often characterised by an artificial positivity as they struggle never to allow a 'bad' feeling to arise. Feelings are natural and proper. A fully functioning person has a full range of feelings. The belief, overt or implicit, that enlightenment will be reached when we only get emotions of one particular kind or when 'bad' feelings have been eliminated is a kind of madness and quite untrue. The role of the therapist may often be to help educate a person about the normality of emotion and to support them when their quite natural and appropriate feelings arise in response to present or remembered events. One client of mine who had been in a psychiatric hospital for a long time and who was now gradually returning to normal life came to me one day and said: 'I have been crying all weekend ... and I know you will be pleased.' She was right. This was a person who had been unable to tolerate any of the feelings of distress which were, nonetheless, quite appropriate to her reflections upon her tragic history.

The person who is out of touch with their feelings usually needs help in amplifying the stimulus and in reducing the distance between themselves and the reality of their lives. We all use a variety of techniques for distancing ourselves. The therapist or spiritual friend may counter this by dramatising the events, using very direct language and adding appropriate intonation to statements which have originally been presented 'flat'. The methods of many humanistic and existential therapies such as person-centred therapy, gestalt and psychodrama may all play a part here[2] just as do the dramatic actions of some Buddhist teachers.

Much Buddhist ritual is specifically designed to add a charge of emotional significance to ordinary events, like taking a meal or drinking tea. The use of beauty, drama and visual effects is all part of the attempt to bring the person to a more intense quality of life in which feelings and actions are fully integrated. When skilfully used, ritual is moving and transformative, reaffirming the connection between the particular individual experience and the larger drama in which we all share. Sometimes, on a retreat, we enact a ritual which we call the Lotus Ceremony. Participants have the opportunity to say goodbye to those they have lost. Even the most sceptical members of the group are usually deeply moved when their turn comes to participate. To enact such a personal yet universal drama in the company of a large number of other people is a healing experience. For people to take turns during the ritual at being both 'person in need' and 'person offering help' is especially therapeutic. It requires us to be in touch with our affliction, to allow the passion of grief to rise in us *and* to contain that passion while we care for others and collectively honour the realities of human life. It affirms our sense of common purpose in compassion for one another and for the world at large. Ritual, properly employed, is a therapeutic reaffirmation of the meaning and mystery of life.

It would be quite mistaken to believe that an advanced spiritual person does not feel much. This error would be further compounded if it led to our trying to avoid the arising of natural sentiments within ourselves. That would be most unhealthy. The enlightened people I have met all seem to me to be very human and complete characters with feelingful personalities. The rapprochement between spirituality and psychotherapy which is emerging in the Buddhist world is, I hope, a good sign that we are on the way to banishing this fallacy.

The Pleasure Trap

The Buddha is quite specific. He says that the thirst that arises with affliction directs itself toward one of three objectives and in the Third Noble Truth, which we shall come to shortly, he advises us to let go of these objectives completely. To let go of the objectives, however, is not the same as letting go of the feelings themselves. The three objectives are that we either seek pleasure, or we seek a different life, or we seek oblivion. These three strategies he later refers to by the simpler terms 'greed, hate and delusion'.

According to Buddhist psychology each of these three urges is itself conditional in three ways. Each feeling has a cause, a provocation and an object. The cause lies within us and is a product of our past. The provocation is the affliction encountered in the present. The object is what the impulse fixes upon and drives us toward.

Let us consider an example. A person comes home from a difficult day at the office full of unpleasant feelings. The cause lies in her inner world which has been shaped by her past experience, the decisions she has made and the actions she has engaged in over many years in the past, all of which have left traces in her present mentality. The provocation occurred at the office and will be some aspect of what the Buddha called dukkha: she did not get what she wanted, she lost something, she was associated with people she did not want to identify with, her hopes were thwarted in some way. The object, in this case, may be the bottle of gin on the sideboard.

We can see from this brief analysis that there is no direct relationship between the object and the cause. The Buddha therefore advised us to let go of the former if we are to engage

77

in doing something about the latter. We will return to this method in due course. First, let us look at greed, hate and delusion individually. Greed or pleasure-seeking behaviour, is compensatory. If we believe that we should not have to meet affliction, then we consider its arrival to be, in some way, unfair. We therefore seek compensation by looking for treats.

To seek pleasure is to seek a change in the sensation. We want to be distracted. We look for a more compelling sensation that will pull our attention away from what ails us. Thus, a very common habit for many people when trouble or anxiety arises is to eat excessively. We think that the pleasure of eating will make us feel better and, temporarily, like the burning sensation for the leper, it does. Over-eating, however, does not do us any good. It assuages the feeling within us in the short run, but it is no solution and it has harmful side effects.

Over-eating is not the only behaviour of this type. Sex can also be misused, as can entertainment. We crave for a distraction from the affliction in our lives and grasp onto something that may offer temporary relief. It is at these times however, that we are vulnerable to being seriously hurt. Many people become involved in quite unsuitable relationships, for instance, simply because they could not bear being alone or could not face the grief of a previous loss. It is when we are in flight from affliction that we do ourselves the most serious psychological and, sometimes, physical injury.

The spiritual paths are not immune to this problem either. There are many people who have somehow come to believe that living a spiritual life will obviate the need to grieve or face suffering. This idea is, unfortunately, quite common among Buddhists. In the western religious traditions, the most famous example is St Augustine. Augustine suffered the devastating effects of a bereavement early in his life. Later on he discovered Christianity. Christianity put him in touch with the ultimate dimension of existence. He had great faith. Nonetheless, when, subsequently, his mother died, he suffered the same pain of grief again. At this point he was thrown into confusion because he had believed that having faith would mean that this pain would not happen again. He felt a failure. Faith, however, does not abolish grief. Faith gives us the courage to face adversity with dignity. When we do so, it becomes an experience that strengthens our spirit and returns us to reality. By the Second Noble Truth, the Buddha is telling us that grief is natural, not ignoble. Loss is dukkha. Grief is samudaya. Both are Noble Truths.

The idea that spirituality will be a kind of insurance policy which will ensure that we never have to experience grief again is spiritual greed. All religions have some elements of this. When, early in the sixth century, the Buddhist teacher Bodhidharma arrived in China, he was received by the Emperor. The Emperor told Bodhidharma about all the good works he had done: building monasteries and hospitals, caring for the sick and the poor and supporting religious teachers and ceremonies. He then asked Bodhidharma to assess the merit accumulated by these acts. Bodhidharma shocked the Emperor by saying that, although he had undoubtedly brought some good and happiness into the world, he had missed the real point of Buddhism, an aspect of which was to be empty of the desire for reward. Much of what passes for religion and spirituality is actually a kind of spiritual materialism in which the search for treats is just as keen as that of a child in a sweet shop.

The fact is that we never know what is round the next corner. Surprise requires spirit. Whatever we encounter, we can meet it with fullness of spirit. The last thing we want is to be unmoved by what we meet on our journey. If meeting affliction had not roused his spirit, the Buddha would never have taught his Dharma. The point of the Dharma is not to substitute one kind of indulgence for another. The point is to help us lead noble lives that make a difference.

There is always affliction of some kind. The body, for instance, is never completely at ease. If we turn our attention to it, we realise that there is always some tension. Often, however, these discomforts are blanked out by the more generalised tension that we live with all the time. We are not awake to our own process. Obstacles wake us up. Enlightenment does not abolish them – it is dependent upon them.

Dukkha is a spark. Samudaya is fire. Fire is both a blessing and a curse. On the one hand, it is dangerous. On the other hand, we would be very cold without it. Sometimes the fire is easy to see. Sometimes, however, the fire may be burning in a different room of our house from the one we are in and this hidden fire may be out of control. We are unaware of the destruction that is going on. Many people live in burning houses of this kind.[2]

In the second major presentation of his teachings the Buddha offered a discourse called The Fire Sermon.[3] A little time after his conversion of the five ascetics, he stayed with a community of fire worshippers. In the teaching he gave to them he pointed out that every single sensation which we experience, whether through the eye, the ear, the tongue, the nose, through touch or even through imagination, is a spark. There is no way that the fire will cease to burn, because we encounter it anew every moment. In the Fire Sermon the Buddha says that we need to be able to stand back from this process sufficiently so that we can see what is going on. Then we can be in command. We can use the fire rather than being consumed by it. The Fire Sermon does not say that the fire should be extinguished. The point is not to put out the fire, but to make it useful.

As a psychotherapist I spend much of my time listening carefully to people. As I tune in to them a kind of resonance starts to occur. I feel something of what they feel. As they describe what concerns them, I imaginatively accompany them. As I imagine myself in their shoes, I begin to feel similar 'arisings' in myself to those that they experience. This experience of empathic resonance is well known to psychotherapists and counsellors. It takes a certain amount of training, however, to realise that these are not simply 'my own feelings' even though I am really feeling them. When I realise that they are not mine, then noticing what is arising in me gives me very helpful information about the suffering of the client.

This phenomenon of resonance is created by my imaginatively imitating the client's process. I do not imagine the client's feeling. I imagine the things in the client's experience that give rise to their feeling. When I do so a real feeling arises in me. I really do feel the anger or sadness or desire or fear or whatever it is. I really feel it and I know that it is not mine. I have become a container for it. By imaginatively replicating the conditions (the affliction) that impinge upon the client, precisely the same samudaya occurs in me as is occurring in them.[4]

This experience of becoming a container for feelings which have been triggered by listening emphatically to somebody else's story also enables us to learn that we are containers for the feelings triggered by our own story. Even when the feelings are my own, in the sense that they relate to events in my own life, it is still possible for me to regard them with a degree of dispassion at the same time as they are occurring: not too close and not too far away.[5]

This ability to be both in and aside from the feeling, at the same time is something that the Buddha taught his disciples to cultivate. He did not teach them to not have feelings. He taught them to allow the process to flow whilst also being able to observe it. The flow of feelings gives us essential information about our lives. To cut them off would be one extreme – the extreme of asceticism. To abandon ourselves to their control would be the other extreme – the extreme of indulgence. The Buddha taught a Middle Way between these extremes, a middle current where life flows effectively. This teaching of observing feeling *while in the feelings* is given time and again in the Buddha's basic instructions on mindfulness.[6]

· 13 ·

Hate and Delusion

If the first form of craving is greed for things that may distract us, then the second form is the desire for a different life. This may be directed inwardly or outwardly. When it is directed inwardly, we blame ourselves for our failure to be perfect. When it is directed outwardly, we blame others. Terry suffers from a disease which causes her body to shake. The best medical care has failed to control the shaking. Disease is dukkha. Her condition is a fact about which she can do little. Relaxation exercises help, but they do not eliminate the trouble. It is very easy for Terry to blame herself for her inability to be just like everyone else and this can sap her confidence terribly. It is also easy for her to become full of anger about her situation. When this happens she blames everybody who has a role in her life, including those who help her, as well as those who really have hurt her. Blaming herself and blaming others, however, simply make her more tense and when she is tense she shakes more, sometimes exhausting herself. Terry has a good deal to feel angry about, but the disease is only aggravated by the anger she feels. There is no point in blaming Terry either! What she needs is understanding from others and acceptance from herself. The disease itself, however, is not going to go away.

Next door to Terry there lives a woman, Mary, who suffers from diabetes. One day Terry realised that Mary had not been seen for some time. After some enquiries Mary was found in her bathroom having collapsed, suffering from low blood sugar. Terry took charge of the situation and got Mary to hospital with efficiency and calm. Even though Terry spends much time brooding upon her own failings and lack of confidence, when action was required she proved quite capable.

One day a woman came to see the Buddha carrying her dead baby. She was called Kisagotami. She asked the Buddha for medicine to heal her baby. The Buddha sent her to fetch some mustard seed which, he said, had to be obtained from a household where nobody had died. As Kisagotami went round the village looking for the seed, she heard about the suffering of every family. Every household had its particular grief. Everybody was suffering. Even though most people pretended that all was well, each had their painful secret. In the end, Kisagotami gave up her search for the medicine which would heal her child. The cure for her grief was not found in achieving her wish that things be different and her child be restored. The cure was found in acceptance of the universality of loss and the growth of compassion for others.

Of course, when suffering strikes, our first desire is for the situation to be different. When we suffer a loss, the first thing we are inclined to do is to deny that it has happened. 'This cannot be real', we tell ourselves. Then the next thing that happens is that we feel angry. We try to escape by blaming others, but the blaming generally makes the situation worse. We may blame the people we live with, our job, our parents, our society, the government, our bodies or even ourselves.

In psychotherapy, it has become fashionable to blame the parents. It is very easy to lay all our troubles at their door. After all, if it was not for them, we would not have been born in the first place. They loved us too little or too much. They were cruel and did not understand. They were selfish. They were human. However much we blame them and however true the complaints we assail them with, blaming keeps us hooked and gets in the way of constructive living. Our parents are, for good or for ill, in us. We have to reach a reconciliation. If we do not do so we will go on tearing ourselves apart. Respect for ourselves is a function of the respect we have for others. Respect sets us free.

When we blame, this is what the Buddha calls a craving to become something else or someone else. We wish that our life were different. Really we wish that we were not exposed to affliction and we falsely believe that if we had a different life in a different time and place where we were not associated with this husband or this wife or these children or these parents or this job or house or body or whatever, then dukkha would not reach us. Of course this is not true. The form of dukkha might be different, but dukkha there would be. Blame, like greed, gives us a temporary respite, but it does not improve our life. Quite the contrary. Blame is the fire getting out of control. If we let the wind catch it, such fires can burn down everything that is capable of giving us happiness and peace. Where greedy behaviour damages us slowly and insidiously, hateful behaviour can unleash a terrible fire storm that can do great damage in a short time.

DELUSION

Attachment and aversion are two short term strategies. There is a third. Some people reach for the bottle. It may be a bottle of alcohol or a bottle of pills, but the effect is much the same. Quite a large proportion of the population find it difficult to bear even one day without the effect of alcohol. Much of the agricultural land in the world is devoted exclusively to the production of alcohol – and this while others starve. Yet alcohol does much physical damage to our bodies and leads to socially destructive behaviour. Of course, oblivion is not sought solely through drinking. Many other drugs are used – many of them nowadays prescribed by doctors. Oblivion is an accepted 'solution' for many people. The ultimate oblivion-seeking behaviour is suicide. Where hateful behaviour can do massive damage in a short time and greedy behaviour has a slow undermining effect upon our lives, behaviour based on the desire for oblivion does both. We suffer in the short run and we suffer in the long run. This is the most extreme form of escapism. The attempt to destroy suffering in this way, however, destroys us.

We are all aware of the destructive effects of alcohol, heroin and opiates. There is, however, another form of seeking for oblivion of which we should also beware. This is the search for a spiritual oblivion. The manner in which nirvana, the goal of Buddhist practice, is commonly portrayed, is just such an oblivion. This led Freud, for instance, to the comment that, 'The Nirvana principle expresses the trend of the death instinct.'[1] I am sure this was not the Buddha's intention. This idea of nirvana as oblivion is part of the cosmology that says that we are going round and round through life after life and all lives are miserable, so the only solution is to stop living altogether. This seems to have been a widely held view in India. I do not think that this is what the Buddha taught but, given the prevalence of the idea in the culture he lived in, it would not be surprising if some of this idea got imported into the Buddhist tradition.

The word nirvana is commonly and I suggest, mistakenly, taken to indicate the going out of a fire. In fact the word means 'without-wind'. *Nir* means 'out of' or 'without'. *Va* means 'wind'. The interpretation of this word as 'extinction' assumes that the 'wind' in question is our life. However, I think a quite different image is intended. Wind is what makes fires dangerous. Everybody who listened to the Buddha would have understood this. We need the fire, but we need it under control. A fire extinguished is no use to anybody.

NOT BLIND TO CAUSALITY

The Buddha was enlightened. His fire was very hot and it was under control. He was full of life and we still feel the vibrancy of his spirit echoing down the centuries. It was not all easy going however. Often the Buddha is depicted in the texts conversing with *Mara*. *Mara* means death. What this indicates is that the Buddha sees the temptation to let the fire die. An enlightened life inevitably involves a dialogue with death. When death triumphs within life, we speak of demoralization and the Buddha spoke of defeat. The Buddha taught the way to avoid defeat. He is often referred to as 'the victor'. This does not mean that the Buddha aims to live forever, however. Death has its proper time. The Buddha is awake to causality and therefore accepts that the body will die.

In the year 1228 a Chinese Zen Master Wumen Huikai published a collection of stories about real and mythical Zen Masters of the past. Each story illustrates some aspect of enlightenment. The book is called *Wumenguan*.[2] The title is a play on words which can be translated several different ways such as 'Wumen's Border Pass' or 'The Pass with no Barrier'. An implication of the title is that the problem is not what you think it is. This is a direct allusion to the Buddha's original teaching that dukkha is not the problem. The stories in Wumen's book have come to be called *koans*.[3] They were intended for use by Zen trainees to help them penetrate to the real meaning of Buddhist teaching. Each story illustrates some aspect of Buddhist understanding.

The second story in Wumen's book relates directly to the Second Noble Truth. It is called 'The Fox'. Here is the relevant section of the story:

> An old man came to listen to Master Baizhang's talks. One day the old man stayed on afterwards. The old man told Baizhang that he was not a human being but lived on the mountain as a fox. This plight had befallen him because he had, in a former life, told a disciple that spiritually advanced people are not subject to causality. As a result, he had been a fox for five hundred lifetimes. Now he wanted to be released. He therefore asked Baizhang: 'Are spiritually advanced people still subject to causality?' The master said: 'They are not blind to causality.' The old man was enlightened.

Many people get involved in spiritual practice, as we have seen, because they want to escape. They want to be 'free from causality'. No doubt Buddhism has become popular because many people believe that it offers this prospect. This is not, however, at all what it is about. Those who teach that the Buddha shows us a way to avoid causality are just crafty foxes. Being free from causality would mean that in a buddha the fire is extinguished. It would mean that when a buddha encountered affliction he or she would feel nothing. The Buddha, however, did not become immune to causality, he became alert to it. By becoming alert to it he became free. He was then no longer burdened and could live happily in the real world, dying at the right time and not before. Buddhism does not offer an escape into a metaphysical paradise. It offers the opportunity to become master of the fire.

Part 4
Character

Taming the Fire

The Third Noble Truth is *Nirodha*. This word means to 'confine'. *Rodha* originally meant an earth bank. *Ni* means 'down'. The image is of being down behind a sheltering bank of earth or of putting a bank around something so as to both confine and protect it. Here again we are talking about the art of controlling a fire.[1]

It is natural that the Buddha should have used the image of fire so much. Fire is a natural symbol for passion, in our language as much as in his own. It was particularly relevant, however, in ancient India since the image of the holy man that most people were familiar with was of the priest who kept a fire. The common religious practice of the Buddha's day was sacrifice to the fire god Agni. The priests of Agni had a fire. Offerings were brought by the faithful. The priest lived off the offerings and the worshippers believed that their sacrifice appeased the god and brought good fortune. The Buddha had a rather poor view of this common practice which involved slaughtering animals, supported priests who were not particularly virtuous and cultivated an attitude of spiritual greed. For the public, however, looking after a fire was the job of the religious. The Buddha's monks did not tend physical fires, like the priests of Agni, but the language of fire and the language of religion were intertwined, nonetheless

Control of fire was, in the early stages of civilisation, a major human achievement. We know how important fire was to people at this stage of the development of technology from the ancient Greek myth of Prometheus. Prometheus was punished by the Olympian gods in the most terrible way. They tied him to a rock where his entrails would be torn out by birds of prey every day. At night they were magically restored so that he could suffer the same torment again the following day. What was the crime that Prometheus had committed? He had taken fire from Olympus and given it to humans. Mastery of fire made humans virtually into gods. Fire provides power. Modern civilisation too depends upon our control over energy. So fire is immensely useful and also dangerous. There is a close association between the word fire and the idea of spirit. There is also a close association between fire and emotion or passion. Spirituality is the art of mastering our fire.

This imagery, therefore, would be readily understandable to ordinary people in the Buddha's day. People cooked their food over a fire. Fire was both useful and dangerous. A fire out of control was a terrible thing. A fire under control was immensely useful. The thing that made a fire dangerous was wind. Unless a fire is protected from the wind it can get out of control very quickly. To keep a fire under control, therefore, you build a bank of earth on the windward side at least, if not all the way round. To get the most useful fire of all, you confine it almost completely by constructing an oven. Nirvana means safe from the wind. Nirodha means to protect the fire from the wind and so render it safe and useful.

If you want to be able to use a fire for cooking or for smelting metal, then you do not want a disorderly blaze which is all smoke and flame. You want a concentrated hotbed of coals. To build a fire of that kind means confining the heat so that you can regulate the draught and not let energy escape too fast. This image provides an excellent metaphor for what the Buddha had in mind. He was aware that people have great torrents of energy which could be put to good use in the creation of a better world. All too often, however, this energy is frittered away on trivia or, worse, goes into conflict and destruction. He wanted us to harness this energy.

The First Noble Truth tells us that the arising of trouble is not something that we can ever wholly avoid. Even the Buddha met with many obstacles, including physical injury, assassination attempts, problems with his relatives, division amongst his disciples, the deaths of his friends and patrons and, eventually, his own illness and death from food poisoning. His life was not smooth and trouble-free. But he did live it to the full. He did not go through it merely existing. He did not take the things that happened as more or less than they were. If he suffered an injury, he felt the pain. He felt the pain, but he did not go into a downward spiral of anguish. He did not see the injury as a sign of his bad luck, for instance. He did not start to feel self-pity or take this as indicating that he was ill-fated or one of life's victims. The body is prone to injury. If an injury occurs, this is not really out of the ordinary. Getting injured from time to time is part and parcel of having a body. He had feelings. He did not exaggerate them nor did he diminish them.

When the Buddha's friend King Bimbisara was condemned to death by his son, I am sure the Buddha felt sad. He felt compassion for the king who had to die a painful death by starvation. He also felt compassion for Bimbisara's son Ajatashattru who was, in his own folly, making himself into a murderer, storing up untold anguish for himself in years to come and setting a gruesome precedent. Ajatashattru was later murdered by his own son in turn. The Buddha felt the impact of these terrible things, but he was not led by them into actions which made the situation worse. A great being like the Buddha is great precisely because he is able to weather even the most terrible events without being panicked into acting in ways which create further trouble. He or she has a big mind, a big heart, which, like a big expanse of water, can swallow even the biggest boulders which fall into it, without the splash creating a tidal wave. Small beings, people with no spiritual resilience, are quite the opposite. Because their minds are small and closed, even a little pebble falling into their pond makes a great splash and disturbs them to the point where they feel at the limit of endurance. Small hurts are quickly magnified into major crises as little things are taken to be signs of bigger ones.

With the Third Noble Truth we notice a change in the tone of the Buddha's statements. He says 'What is the Noble Truth of confinement? It is the complete confinement of that thirst. It is to let go of, be liberated from and refuse to dwell in the object of that thirst.' The difference between this statement and the statements about the first two Noble Truths is that here there is something for us to do. The first two Truths tell us that there are certain things that are unavoidable. The last two tell us that there are, nonetheless, some things that we can and should do. To have spirit means both to have some fire and to keep it under control. It means to accept and not be defeated by what we can do nothing about. It also means to rise to the challenge of doing what does need to be done.

In this imagery, the Buddha identifies greed, hate and delusion as being like wind blowing the mind out of control, so that, like a windswept fire, it uses up its fuel too quickly and to no purpose, dissipating itself (greed), causing damage (hate) and going out (delusion). According to Buddhist psychology each impulse of the mind has a cause created in the distant past, a provocation in the immediate past and an object which it impels us toward. In the fire metaphor, the cause is the inflammable quality of the sticks: the presence of fuel. The provocation is the spark. A spark would have no effect if the fuel were not present and ready. The outward flow of mind toward objects is impelled by the dangerous wind of greed, hate and delusion. The Buddha does not, contrary to received opinion, advise us never to start fires. Without fire we will get nowhere, but the fire has to be cared for skilfully. The fuel is all the material that is stored away in our karmic storehouse. Everything we have ever done has left its mark upon us. We are therefore inevitably prone to ignite when the right spark occurs. We are a fire waiting to happen. This in itself is no bad thing. A person who was never lit up by life would be dull indeed. The test of character is how well we use and direct the resulting fire.

Potentially, we are all riders of great dragons. The dragon is a fire animal. In fairy stories the hero has to either get the better of the dragon or get the assistance of the dragon. The former plot is typical of western fairy stories. The dragon ends up dead. In eastern fairy stories the outcome is more commonly that the hero gains the help or favour of the dragon. A dragon's scale becomes a magic aid bestowed by the dragon in token of the hero's virtue or courage and it conveys special protection and power. The spirit of Buddhism is not to kill the dragon. Dragons are immortal. The Buddhist approach is to befriend the fire animal and so gain the benefit of its power which can then be used for good in the world. The fire animal is within ourselves.

Western religions have often sought to kill off the dragon within us. That would not be the spirit of Buddhism. The spirit of Buddhism is to ride the dragon.

I therefore reject the idea that nirvana means the extinction of the fire. Extinction does seem to have been the goal for some of the indigenous religions of India, but it was not the Buddha's aim. Far from achieving extinction, the Buddha set turning a wheel which is still gathering momentum twenty-five centuries later. He lived an active, creative life, full of lively relationships, controversy and innovation. If his aim really was extinction, then he could not have failed to achieve it more comprehensively. Dharma is not about destroying the energy of our passion, nor repression. It is, rather, about the conscious direction of the energy. It is about harnessing, not destroying. Nirodha means to capture, not to destroy. By capturing fire, mankind was able to create civilisation. By capturing our own inner fire, we will transform the world.

As long as we are at the mercy of the winds of greed, hate and delusion, we will continue to create injustice, oppression and cruelty, however much we may believe that we are good civilised citizens. By becoming masters of our fire, however, we become *bodhisattvas*, awakened beings capable of working for the real good of the world. Such a person has character. They have spiritual fire and they have it well sheltered so that it is at their command. I have been fortunate to meet many people like this, people who have pursued the path of Buddhist training and become great dragons.

The people I have in mind, people like Jiyu Kennett Roshi, Akong Rimpoche, Chogyam Trungpa and Thich Nhat Hanh have not been particularly conventional souls. They are not conformist. They are innovators. They have fire in their belly and peace on their lips. They are constructive. When the wind blows, they become uncannily still, poised. When the wind dies down they move with great decisiveness. The world needs more people like this.

Kondañña was so happy when he understood this principle because he saw straight away that the Buddha was describing something he could do. For years and years he had been trying to do something that he could not do, which was to stop dukkha arising in the first place and to stop craving arising in his heart. He had been trying to put the fire out. Now he discovered that he could use the fire itself. This prospect made him very pleased. There was no need to destroy a part of himself. It is very easy for people to make the mistake of believing that to be spiritual means to discriminate between what is good and what is bad and then to eliminate all that is bad. Real spirituality goes well beyond that kind of moralism. The task of spirituality is to channel energy rather than destroy it. When Kondañña understood, he knew that the impulses which he had formerly regarded as bad were actually simply further sources of energy which could be applied to the holy life. They could now be welcomed rather than feared.

The impulses of the mind come from a place beyond our conscious control. To set oneself to prevent their arising is either to sentence oneself to death or to attempt the impossible. As long as the mind is alive, cravings of one sort or another will arise. A noble practitioner of the spiritual path, however, sees them arise and sees how to harness them. This is possible and practical. It offers a genuinely workable path for ongoing practice. Dukkha is noble. The fire in us is noble. Mastery of the fire is noble. The path is noble. Kondañña became enlightened to this path and so can we.

The Buddha says that the way to confine the energy of feelings is not by suppressing the feeling, but by detaching from the object of the feeling. This is an immensely important distinction. Feelings are all, in some sense, cravings or thirsts. Craving, or thirst, is always craving for something. What lies behind craving is affliction. When craving arises, however, we do not ordinarily look at the affliction itself, we look at the object of our craving which does not necessarily have any direct connection with the cause of affliction at all. The mind that is suffering is pleased to be distracted and so flows out to whatever is to hand. The person who has had a difficult day at the office reaches for the bottle of gin. This outflow toward such an object has to be restrained if we are to see into our nature. This outflow is the wind that can whip the fire out of our control. The Buddha's prescription, therefore, is that we should learn to be sufficiently awake to what is happening that when a craving arises we should be able to unhook ourselves from the object of the impulse. It requires an effort to restrain the hand that reaches for the bottle, but that effort is well invested if it is accompanied by a serious intention to become aware of the real driving factor in the situation.

We do not generally see the suffering inside us. We only see the object of our desire. What the Buddha suggests we give up is not the desire itself, but the object toward which it is directed. To do so enables us to turn around and see what we are running away from. Slipping another biscuit into our mouth in a mindless way just dissipates the energy that the Buddha would have us conserve for the great work. The enemy of enlightenment is dissipation.

As soon as we feel ourselves attaching to an object, we can be sure that there is some suffering that we are trying to escape. The object may be something physical, like a cake, or it may be another person, or it may be a circumstance we desire, like promotion at work. Spiritual practitioners learn to unhook themselves from the object of their desire. By doing so, they create stillness without destroying the passion. Inner stillness and inner fire co-exist. The fire is protected

In this stillness we may be able to look inside and see what we are escaping from. To do so is therapy. This element of therapy is not essential to the spiritual process. The Four Noble Truths do not go so far. They simply show us the relationship between passion and awakening. Nonetheless, the insights come as we attend to our passion within the stillness. The client in psychotherapy also learns to let go of the object of compulsive behaviour and, fortified by the accompaniment of the therapist, turn to look at the suffering they are carrying. The therapist provides protection. In psychotherapy, the therapist acts like the bank of earth protecting the client's fire. In time, the client learns to perform this function for themselves: to rely upon their own spirit.

Nirodha is the pivotal spiritual exercise of the Buddhist path. We can apply it whenever we feel compulsive desires rising in us. If we do not do so, we may be swept away. If we try simply not to have any passion in the first place, we will never amount to much.

Of course, there are also people who make their suffering itself the object of their attachment. It becomes the focus of all their thought. Rumination then becomes a way of life. In his talk, therefore, the Buddha simply says that the Third Noble Truth is a matter of 'the complete confinement of that thirst. It is to let go of, be liberated from and refuse to dwell in the object of that thirst.' To become aware of and understand the dukkha which is the source of energy in our lives is valuable. To become aware of and nurture the passion to which it gives rise is also valuable. To let that energy flow away into trivial distractions or petty feuding is lamentable. It is like going to a lot of trouble to get something and then wasting it all.

The Dharma practitioner, therefore, does not go to the extreme either of drowning in sorrow or of ignoring suffering. There is a Middle Way more spirited than either of these back waters. When we notice craving arising we notice what it is directed toward, unhook ourselves and conserve the energy for the practice of the higher path. We may notice what suffering lies behind the impulse or we may not know what is fuelling our passion. Nonetheless, we respect it.

· 15 ·

Spirit without Metaphysics

When we looked at the First Noble Truth, we came to understand it in a way that was different from the orthodox interpretation. We discovered that it is not about the necessity to abolish suffering, but about the needlessness of our shame about suffering. Since then we have examined the Second and Third Noble Truths. Here again we have arrived at conclusions very different from the standard ones found in most books about Buddhism. The common explanation is that the Second Truth tells us that dukkha arises *as a result* of craving and that the Third Truth tells us how dukkha ceases with the extinction of craving. The implication of this common interpretation is a belief that all dukkha can be abolished by abolishing craving. This is what many people do try to do and it is this strategy which defeats them. Many people try to control the arising of their feelings and think this is the way to control their lives. When it does not work, they consider themselves failures or think it is a matter of just trying harder or longer.

We have seen some of the problems inherent in the common interpretation and we have been exploring a quite different approach. Since dukkha includes such things as birth, ageing and death, the principle that dukkha ceases when craving ceases leads by a direct process of logic to the idea that when craving ceases, mortal life ceases. Since the Buddha did not die immediately after his enlightenment nor become an immortal, some further explanation is required. One idea is that the Buddha went on living for another forty-five years in order to use up the last vestiges of karmic imperfection that still hung around him from his former existences. This idea is widely accepted, but seems rather unsatisfactory. If the Buddha really did achieve complete enlightenment and if the effect of enlightenment is to bring craving to an end and if the effect of craving ceasing is dukkha ceasing, it seems illogical that the Buddha continued to experience all those years of dukkha after his awakening. Is the fruit of enlightenment only really experienced after death? This seems both improbable and out of kilter with the general tone of the Buddha's teaching.

The idea that craving creates dukkha and the end of craving eliminates dukkha and that this effectively terminates the basis of life has, however, become an established doctrine in most schools of Buddhism through the teaching on rebirth. In fact, if you take the common interpretation of the Second and Third Noble Truths as correct, it is very difficult to avoid the conclusion that birth in this life must be the result of craving in a previous life and that craving in this life will be the cause of rebirth in a future life. If birth is dukkha and dukkha is caused by craving, then the craving must have occurred before birth.

The standard interpretation is thus indissolubly linked to the idea of rebirth. It culminates in the idea that the end of craving leads to the end of the circle of rebirths. The Four Noble Truths are thus made the basis for a metaphysical doctrine about cycles of life after life. On this interpretation the supreme achievement of the Buddha was that he reached the point where he would not have to be reborn again in the literal sense. The implication of this doctrine of rebirth and freedom from rebirth is that the best thing you can do with this life is escape from it. I have never been happy with this interpretation which seems to me to go against the grain of the Buddha's intention that we should live happy and satisfying lives here and now. It would also be quite at odds with my interpretation of the First Noble Truth. There is not much that one could call noble in running away or seeking extinction.

Another problem which arises with the standard interpretation is the nature of nirvana. A very lucid account of the standard interpretation is given by Walpola Rahula in his popular book, *What the Buddha Taught*. This is what he has to say about the Third Truth: 'The Third Noble Truth is that there is emancipation, liberation, freedom from suffering, from the continuity of *dukkha*. This is . . . *Nirvana*. To eliminate *dukkha* completely one has to eliminate the main root of *dukkha*, which is "thirst"'.[1] He then immediately goes on, 'Now you will ask: But what is Nirvana? ... The only reasonable reply to give to the question is that it can never be answered completely and satisfactorily in words, because human language is too poor to express the real nature of the Absolute Truth or Ultimate Reality which is Nirvana.'

Why is it said to be so difficult for us to understand what nirvana is? I do not think the Buddha would have been reticent in this way. I think that he chose words with the intention of being understood, words that would be meaningful for ordinary people he met. Nirvana is a word he used all the time and he clearly intended people to understand what he was talking about. What has happened is that the idea of nirvana has got muddled up with ideas about a state of sublime reward which exists *after death*, rather than being a useful term which conjures up a familiar image relevant to everyday life. Nirvana has become identified with an 'Absolute Truth or Ultimate Reality', written with initial capital letters. In fact nirvana was something that the Buddha said was immediately available to all of us here in this very life simply by penetrating into the full implication of the Noble Truths and putting them into practice. Nirvana is not a metaphysical entity. I suggest that it is a practical term describing the art of mastering the fire within us. This is a metaphor which would be transparent to ordinary people. It does not require belief in ultimates and absolutes. It points not toward metaphysics, but toward practice.

My suggestion therefore, is that the whole teaching of rebirth is unnecessary to a proper understanding of the Four Noble Truths and that these Truths are not concerned with the way to bring an end to a succession of circlings through many incarnations which is basically a Hindu idea not a Buddhist one. They are really concerned with how to live happily in the midst of this very life, just as it is. I do not say that rebirth is true, nor that it is false. Perhaps there is some way to establish whether we do survive death as distinct entities or not. Or perhaps there is no way to do so. Rebirth or no, what the Buddha is saying makes sense in terms of this life. If there are future lives, it will make sense there, too. It is not, however, necessary to have a belief in rebirth to make sense of the Buddha's message.

This is further evidenced by the fact that Kondañña was enlightened there and then. The common interpretation leads to the conclusion that becoming enlightened will take many years or, more likely, many lifetimes. In fact, many current schools of Buddhism seem in practice to be based on the premise that really nobody ever does get enlightened. A mythology has grown up to the effect that enlightenment was only available to people who lived in the Buddha's own time. At that time, apparently, there were gathered in the world many beings who had been preparing to incarnate at that precise moment for many aeons just so they could be present with Buddha Shakyamuni and get enlightened by him. To me, this does not ring true. This is another metaphysical idea and I do not think it accurately represents either the truth or the Buddha's intention. What he taught is just as relevant for us as it was for people in his own day and the possibility of enlightenment is just as present today as then. I myself have met quite a number of enlightened people if we take the term in the way suggested in this book.

Some have criticised my earlier book, *Zen Therapy*, for failing to make clear to the reader that to get anywhere in Buddhism takes a very long time. I did not say that to eliminate craving and dukkha requires many many years of training. The reason that I did not make this point about years and years of training being necessary to achieve the goal of Buddhism is that it is not true. It is not what the Buddha taught and it is not supported by the many stories of people becoming enlightened after a very brief encounter with him. The truth of Buddhism is not about training for thousands of lifetimes. One may gradually cultivate life improvement indefinitely, but enlightenment is sudden.

If the common interpretation of the Four Noble Truths is correct, then, of course, it would take a very long time indeed and enlightenment would be a mirage that constantly eludes us. In fact, I believe that the Buddha was saying that *that* – the elimination of dukkha and samudaya – would indeed take forever. He did not ask that people never experience suffering or craving again. He asked that we open our eyes to the reality of these phenomena in the life of the world, rise above them, harness their energy and live spirited lives. On this path we will

meet many obstacles and personal problems within enlightenment and we will meet them with spirit and character. Our lives
will become of service to the great work and will no longer be
futile nor trivial.

People who accept the common interpretation believe it takes
a long time to get enlightened because they are attempting an
impossible task and whenever they stop to take stock, they
realise that, however much progress they have made, they have
not reached the goal they set for themselves. It does therefore
seem like a very long path. The goal they have set, however, is
not the goal set by the Buddha. The Buddha asked us simply to
understand the situation we are in and to begin putting that
understanding into practice. By doing so we will be able
immediately to let go of the guilt we feel about dukkha and
craving and a great joy will arise in our hearts. This is precisely
what happened to Kondañña. The reason that it did not happen
immediately to the other four ascetics was not that it is an
inherently lengthy process, but simply that they did not fully
grasp the significance of what the Buddha said. They were,
however, sufficiently impressed to enrol as disciples and the
Buddha taught them the methods which he believed might bring
them closer to the necessary insight.

The model presented in this book is: life naturally and
inevitably involves the experience of affliction. Affliction gives
rise to feelings. The energy of feelings can be harnessed if it can
be sheltered from the wind of greed, hate and delusion – 'the
ego wind'. The spiritual life is the path which unfolds when our
energies are tamed in this way.

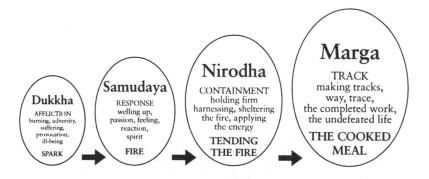

This model is, on the face of it, much more straight forward than the orthodox one. It is in the same linear form as we find in the Buddha's other major teachings and it makes a direct appeal to common sense. If the interpretation given here is correct, then it is quite obvious why the Buddha gave the Four Noble Truths in the order he did. The First leads to the Second. The Second leads to the Third. The Third leads to the Fourth. In the orthodox interpretation this is by no means the case.

Of course, there are two separate issues to be addressed. One issue is whether either of these models accurately represents what the Buddha said twenty-five centuries ago. The other issue is whether either of them is true. The argument of this book is both that the interpretation presented here is what the Buddha really intended and that it is an accurate portrayal of the needs and behaviour of the human spirit. It is also much more in keeping with western psychology and likely to make a more attractive appeal to the western mind than a model rooted in a form of metaphysics alien to western tradition.

One way of testing the truth of a theory is to see what implications it has and to see if these are borne out by observation of the real world. If the orthodox interpretation were true (whether or not it is what the Buddha said), then the spiritual path would be a gradual affair. People would gradually get better and better. As they did so they would experience less and less suffering and exhibit less and less passion. The model presented in this book, by contrast, implies that dukkha is actually the driving force of the path. Dukkha provides the fuel that heats the fire without which the spiritual life would remain feeble. This would suggest that great souls were not necessarily those who had reduced their suffering, nor those whose passions had abated. Great souls would be people who had suffered and, in many cases, continued to suffer, and who had great passion, but had that passion controlled and directed to a worthwhile end. They would be people who had lived.

When we consider people like my own particular collection of heroes: people like Gandhi, Martin Luther King, Nelson Mandela, Mother Theresa, Master Nhat Hanh and even Jesus Christ and the Buddha himself, I think the evidence suggests that these are not people who have avoided dukkha. They are not people who are quietly subsiding, however virtuously. They are people who have had to struggle and overcome great obstacles, both in their own characters and in the world around them. All such people are possessed by great energy which has its source in the sufferings they have experienced and witnessed. Spiritual greatness is not limited to the followers of one creed. What the Buddha taught is true for all beings, whether they have heard of Buddhism or not.

I have often seen examples of people who were living rather unfruitful lives galvanised into action by the arrival of unavoidable hardship. The *Denkoroku* is a Zen text written by Master Keizan in the early fourteenth century.[2] It is both a manual on the art of getting enlightened and a history of the great masters of the Zen school. In it we see that all of these great masters reached enlightenment by facing the suffering in their lives. They were all people of great character. Many of them lived early lives that were not virtuous. Enlightenment came suddenly. Nor did it bring an easy life. Great souls face great struggles, often even more so after their enlightenment than before it.

After a terrible flood in Vietnam, Master Nhat Hanh wrote the following lines:

> *I have come to be with you*
> *to weep with you*
> *for our ravaged land*
> *and broken lives*[3]

Later, after a particularly awful day during the Vietnam War in which several of his friends had been killed he wrote:

> *I hold my face in my two hands.*
> *No, I am not crying.*
> *I hold my face in my two hands.*
> *to keep the loneliness warm –*
> *two hands protecting,*
> *two hands nourishing,*
> *two hands preventing*
> *my soul from leaving me*
> *in anger.*[4]

These are not the words of one who is on the path of extinction. What is being talked of here is the power of the emotion that co-arises with dukkha. In the case of Master Nhat Hanh, that power has been harnessed and channelled into a vast amount of positive work helping refugees, helping the boat people, establishing Dharma centres and bringing a message of peace and love to the west and, particularly, to the very country, America, which was responsible for inflicting much of the devastation which fell into his life. Similar statements could be made about many other advanced spiritual practitioners. Indeed it is this that qualifies them to be called advanced.

The picture that emerges for me is not of Buddhism as a meek and mild path of graduated virtues, but rather of the cutting power of the Buddha's insight that it is only through the experience of suffering that we summon up the energy to do something truly worthwhile with our lives.

· 16 ·

Psychotherapy

According to the interpretation given in the traditional commentaries, the source of all suffering is desire and the whole enterprise of therapy under such a theory would be the elimination of desire. The goal would be to help a person give up all attachment. The goal and the means to it are here both seen as mental processes. The way to achieving this goal would be the application of the Eightfold Path, which may be summarised as consisting of behavioural discipline, meditation practice and the cultivation of insight and wisdom. Even in this traditional form, therefore, I think it is clear that Buddhism is, whatever else it may also be, a psychotherapy. It is a therapy in the sense that it has a theory of how suffering comes about and it has a range of practices designed to alleviate this condition, and it is specifically a psychotherapy in that it sees the mind as playing a crucial role in this process.[1]

Three areas where people tend to see a difference between Buddhism and psychotherapy as the term is currently understood are that the goal of Buddhism is more total, that Buddhism is prescriptive about morality and that therapy is seen as being about feelings, whereas it is commonly believed that Buddhism does not give a very strong place to feelings in the scheme of things.

Certainly the goal of Buddhism is a bold one. Psychotherapy looks for a relative improvement where Buddhism looks for root and branch change in the person. Psychotherapy is concerned with the adjustment of one person in society. Buddhism looks for the renewal of civilisation through the work of transformed individuals. To me, this simply means that Buddhism is a more ambitious psychotherapy than most. Many of the great psychotherapists, like Sigmund Freud or Carl Rogers, finished up bursting out of the confines of the therapy they invented to spend their later years looking at the same questions in a more global way. Jacob Moreno the founder of psychodrama, felt this limitation particularly keenly. He wrote, in 1934, in the opening statement to his major work, *Who Shall Survive?* 'A truly therapeutic procedure cannot have less an objective than the whole of mankind'.

Buddhism is prescriptive about morality. Some therapists believe that a kind of moral relativism in which the therapist does not expose their own ethical position is essential to their art. To this, however, we can say, firstly, that this is by no means true for all psychotherapies and, secondly, that it is not genuinely possible of achievement. Cognitive therapies are directly concerned with changing the client's beliefs, for instance, and all therapies, overtly or covertly, induce the client into a particular way of viewing the human condition. Complete moral relativism is, in any case, destructive of mental health. If we take no stand on anything, then our lives will fall apart. We will be at the mercy of the wind. Ethics are an important part of nirodha: of the bank we erect to shelter us from the forces of destruction. Ethical dilemmas often lie at the root of what drives a person to seek psychotherapeutic help. Buddhism sees ethical behaviour as supporting mental well-being and therefore sees the adoption of ethical behaviours as healthy.

As for the issue of Buddhism and feelings, one of the purposes of this book is to assert that the common view is wrong. The history of Buddhism is full of courageous and colourful people. The idea that Buddhism is emotionally bland is mistaken. Buddhism offers a Middle Way on the question of feelings. Buddhism is not an example of the 'let it all hang out' school, nor is it in favour of repression. It seeks to harness our deepest passions in the service of all that is good and worthwhile and thereby make our short stay upon this earth meaningful and positively consequential. To achieve this we need to cultivate our passion and control it.

While some people are out of touch with or busy suppressing their feelings, others are overwhelmed by them. Sometimes this is because the dukkha that the person has experienced is so terrible that whenever the memory is triggered they become extremely distressed.[2] Sometimes it is not so much that the affliction is terrible as that the person has placed themselves in or fallen victim to a life situation in which their pain is constantly restimulated. Sometimes it is a case of the person not knowing how to keep their feelings in proportion because they are constantly driven by the ego wind: they take everything personally and have no sense of constancy of purpose, other than the self-defeating aim of always trying to feel good.

Feelings are normal, appropriate and 'a good thing'. This does not mean, however, that they are the only good thing. Actions are even more important. If I feel murderous, this does not justify me acting murderously. It is important to recognise the murderous feeling coming up, not least because if I do not do so I may act on it inadvertently. Recognising this aspect of myself gives me the basis for compassion, even toward those who do actually murder people. Compassion depends upon being able to recognise something of the other in ourselves. Even the energy of murderous rage is, once it is unhooked from its current object, something intrinsically wonderful. Potentially it is the fire of enlightenment. It does, however, need to be tamed. It is important for me not to act upon this feeling in an unthinking way.

There are many figures in Buddhist iconography who represent this transformation of wrathful energy in the service of enlightenment. Shiva is the destroyer god in Hinduism. In the hands of the Buddhists, Shiva became Achala, guardian of the Dharma. He looks ferocious, sword in hand, surrounded by flames, with a necklace of skulls. Buddhists ask for Achala's help in the great work of bringing peace to the world. There are many such figures in Buddhist practice. Meditating upon them helps us achieve the necessary inner alchemy.

As a human being, I am capable of sensing the likely consequences of my actions. I do not need to see these in specific detail. I know that murdering somebody is not going to make the world a happier place. It is necessary for me to check myself and to contain my feelings in a nurturing way. If *all* we do is restrain the anger, it is like keeping a wild dog on a leash. Sooner or later the leash will snap. If I restrain the feeling, but continue to identify with it, I will just build up resentment. This is where religion and society can go wrong. Morality as an external system of rules alone, a mere legalism, will not do. The feelings have to be respected, not suppressed.

If the fire is not to get out of control it must be sheltered from the wind. This means unhooking our desire from its immediate object so that we can feel it purely. Anger may rage in us, and we can know it, but we do not hit somebody. Thus we protect the emotion from the effects of the ego. This requires a degree of detachment. We need to learn to be able to say, 'That's interesting, such and such a feeling has come up in me.' This ability is called mindfulness. Mindfulness puts what is happening to us in the context of the higher purpose of life. It is the opposite of the attitude which is only concerned with self. When we think 'What about me?' we are generally losing sight of 'What am I here for?'.

Psychotherapy provides a situation in which such a combination of being in the flow and being detached becomes possible. To examine the feeling while in the feeling, as the Buddha says,[3] is the key to effective psychotherapy. Therapy provides a kind of ritual in which a space is created where it is possible for feelings to be contained. The boundaries of the therapy relationship act as a protective embankment. The space inside becomes a place where the client feels safe to explore what seem like dangerous issues without so much fear. It is a place where the client can learn to handle their fire without getting burnt. There is a direct parallel between contemporary psychological practice and the Buddha's advocacy of containment and protection as the necessary conditions for psychological transformation.

The work of personal growth is not just about getting in touch with feelings. It is also about considering their appropriateness. It may often be necessary to build a protective bank around a particular passion so that it remains appropriate to the situation to which it applies and is not inappropriately amplified by energy flowing from other times and other events earlier in a person's life. When somebody over-reacts it is generally because their experience of contemporary events is contaminated by the hurt they have been carrying which adds a great deal more fuel to the fire than is apparent to the outside observer. The feeling that 'This always happens to me', for instance, is a common sign that we are not just responding to the matter in hand.

Thus one often sees cases of married couples who generate extremes of conflict over rather trivial matters. As soon as one thing goes wrong, feelings escalate out of control. Small things are taken as symptoms of larger ones. Sparks are caught by the wind. Often the spark is something very small, but the conflagration can be huge. To make a successful relationship we need both to kindle and control the blaze. Close relationships are character-building precisely because they bring bliss and adversity into such close proximity. Everything comes into sharper relief. It all matters more.

So, too, in psychotherapy and in spiritual companionship. Through the medium of a special relationship, the sparks of life come into sharper focus. They can be both amplified and contained. It is through intimate non-threatening interaction with another human being that many of the most important lessons in managing our energy are learned. We need spiritual friends.

Time to Stop

The Buddha became enlightened while sitting in meditation. When we sit in meditation we sit still. All manner of things may arise in the mind, but the body remains still. This combines samudaya and nirodha. The fire burns up and is contained. Things arise. I watch them arise and I watch them depart. Meditation is full awareness of everything that comes up, contained within the posture of silent sitting. The posture plays a vitally important part. Enlightenment is practice of the Four Noble Truths and meditation is such a practice. Simply sitting in meditation manifests all four Noble Truths. Sitting up straight in this way, we exhibit the buddha mind. We should not, therefore, think of meditation as a means toward enlightenment. Meditation is not a means. It is the thing itself.

The reason why the Buddha often describes what we need to do in negative terms is that he discovered that the original condition of the mind is perfectly all right. The unconditioned mind delights in the miracle of daily life, enjoys each breath, savours each taste and looks quite naturally with eyes of love. The reason that we experience this bliss only rarely is that we are conditioned through and through. The aim of Buddhist practice is to allow our original nature to function. This original nature is not something we can construct. All through life the ordinary person is trying to construct a security for themselves. The folly is that we try to construct what is freely available to us. Buddhist teachers are, therefore, 'selling water by the river'[1]. What we need is to stop doing what cuts us off from our natural happiness. The essential intervention that is required in our lives is one which can be well described as 'stopping'.

The basic form of meditation which the Buddha taught is

called *shamatha*. This word means 'stopping'. The effect of shamatha is to bring us peace and joy. Shamatha can be a formal meditation practice done sitting in a traditional posture upon a meditation cushion. It can also be an everyday exercise in which we introduce stops into our ordinary activities. Every time we stop in this way we have an interlude of a few moments in which we return our attention to immediate reality.

Learning to stop is very important. When you feel anger, for instance, do absolutely nothing. Do not let yourself be swept away by the wind. Cultivate stillness. Then the energy of the emotion may be added to your spiritual fire and not be dissipated in meaningless and destructive gestures. Return your attention to your breathing and enjoy a few moments of being alive.

At the Vietnamese Buddhist centre called Plum Village in south-west France there are clocks which chime every fifteen minutes. Residents have adopted the practice of stopping every time the clock chimes. This practice may at first seem quite artificial but, simple as it is, it does have a profound effect over the course of a day. The build up of tension which can occur when we rush from one task to another is interrupted every fifteen minutes.

Many people who, like myself, have visited Plum Village, have imported this practice into their lives back at home with good effects. In our house we are fortunate to have a very nice old chiming clock which my wife inherited from her grandfather. The chime of the bell is attractive in itself. When it chimes, we listen. Whatever the task in hand, we stop and pay attention to our breathing and to whatever is immediately before us. In my case, while I am sitting here writing what is in front of me is the grain of the wood of my desk or the pile of books I have been referring to. When I look at these things caringly, I do not just see utilitarian objects. I also sense the love and care that have gone into their making. In the desk is craftsmanship and family history. It was actually made by my father. There is also the tree which once grew in a forest on the other side of the world and whose life came to an end in order for this desk to be made. In the books there is the whole history of civilisation – and, again, trees.

Mindfulness methods may be taught as therapeutic procedures which are of great value.[2] Generally, for instance, a person who gets carried away by emotion will find, if they stop to examine it, that there are a number of stages in the build up of their feelings. Each of these stages is accompanied by physiological changes, such as rising or falling temperature in particular parts of the body, tightness in the chest, muscular tension, as well as more psychological signs such as particular imagery, memories or thoughts. All these things can be observed. A person who learns to observe them gains greatly in self-control. Many clients have been helped in this way.

Stopping grounds us. The Third Noble Truth is the dignity of stopping. When I stop and appreciate my breath for a moment, or really look at the way the sunshine is catching the wall of the building across the street, I am, for a moment at least, no longer 'a writer' nor 'a psychotherapist', nor any of the other identities that require so much maintenance. I am simply whatever it is that registers beauty, stillness and peace. Whatever that is, it is nameless. It is the unconditioned. It is not something to which categories like good and bad, profit and loss, beginning and ending apply. It is not born and it does not die. It is not trying to achieve something, nor get anywhere. It is. That is all. What does it feel like? Such a relief! Bliss comes when we can protect the silence. This is the meaning of the Third Truth.

Meditation on Breathing
1 Sit quietly in a stable meditation posture.
2 Settle the body.
3 Notice the breath. Notice your general condition. If you are drowsy, focus your attention upon the breath at the nostrils. If you are alert, focus your attention upon the rise and fall of the abdomen.
4 Follow each breath from its origin through to completion: all the way in, all the way out.
5 Enjoy the breath. Smile.

If you find that the mind wanders, notice what has come up and then return your attention to the breath.

If you find it very difficult to prevent the mind wandering, count the breaths. Count from one to ten and then count down again from ten to one. Count once for each complete in and out breath. If you lose count, return to one again.

Alternatively, use a mantra such as NA-MO-A-MI-DA-BU, three syllables on the in breath and three on the out breath. You can learn the associated meanings of the mantra you use and this will insure that the practice also serves as a positive affirmation for you.[3]

Meditation on Feelings

1 Begin with meditation on breathing, as above.
2 Without losing consciousness of the breath begin to take stock of what feelings are in you. Do this very slowly so that you still also keep the breath in mind.
3 When you identify a feeling which may be a sensation or an emotion, notice its quality, strength, and position in the body.
4 Smile at your feeling, whatever it is, and resolve to take care of it.
5 Let go of the feeling.
6 Check that you are still following your breathing.
7 Return to step 2.

You may like to use a phrase such as: 'As I breath in I notice a feeling of . . . in me.' 'As I breath out I smile to the feeling of . . . in me.[4]'

Meditation on Impulses

1 Begin with meditation on breathing.
2 Without losing consciousness of the breath, notice how you are conscious of other sounds, smells, sensations and imaginings, arising from within or outside.
3 Notice how each sensation may bring some impulse toward action in you, however slight.
4 Smile at the impulse, whatever it is.
5 Let go of the impulse.
6 Check that you are still following your breathing.
7 Return to step 2.

Meditation on Loving Kindness

1 Begin with any of the previous meditations.
2 Let go of attending to the breath.
3 Bring to mind somebody you care deeply about.
4 Let yourself be filled with the feeling of love.
5 Imagine love radiating out from yourself to the other person in whatever way works for you. You may see it as light rays, or simply sense a warm radiation, or you may imagine enclosing them in a beneficial feeling.
6 Enjoy saturating the image of the other person with loving feelings.
7 Continue for a few minutes.
8 Return to step 3 bringing another person to mind.

Gradually, you can bring to mind people you do not know well, or even people who are your enemies. There may be other feelings present as well as love. Do not worry. Smile at what is there, and continue to cultivate the loving kindness as well.

These exercises are all enlightened action. We see feelings come up in us in response to our awareness of the forms that appear to our mind and we gently but effectively contain these feelings in a nurturing way. This practice puts us in touch with our deeper life and strengthens us against the ravages of greed, hate and delusion. We learn to be still in the midst of all that is going on and we master the fire within us.

· 18 ·

Angulimala

Stopping can transform our life. The most dramatic description of the workings of this Third Truth in the Buddhist literature is probably the conversion of Angulimala.[1] Angulimala was a bandit. He was at large in the area where the Buddha was staying. He was feared by everyone and many people had fled their homes. He wore a necklace upon which he strung a finger from each of the people he had killed. The Buddha set out to meet Angulimala. As he walked along the road into the area where the bandit was reputed to be, people called out to him to stop. Many armed men had been killed. What chance was there for an unarmed monk?

Eventually the Buddha came close to where Angulimala was and the bandit was struck by the audacity of the monk. At first his thought was to kill him, but clearly something gave him pause. Although Angulimala's habit was to kill, he was con- ditioned to kill people who either were fighting him or who were frightened of him. This monk was not behaving in the accustomed manner and so Angulimala did not act in a purely conditioned way. He stopped for a moment to think about the matter. This interuption in the usual flow of conditioned behaviour is the crucial gap that is necessary if some new enlightenment is to occur. There has to be a chink for the light to get in.

Angulimala wanted to regain the sense of command that he usually felt. The monk's unflustered demeanour was unset- tling him. On the other hand, the monk was unarmed and offered no realistic threat. There was no need for haste. He decided to try to reassert himself. He hurried after the Buddha and ordered him to stop. The Buddha then said a remarkable thing. He said 'Angulimala, I *have* stopped. Now it is your turn to stop.'

'What do you mean? You are walking along, yet you say it is I who need to stop.'

Angulimala had failed to regain control of the situation. He now wanted to know what the Buddha meant.

The Buddha said, 'I have stopped harming living beings. You have yet to stop.' Probably the Buddha said more, but this was the gist of it. Real weapons had never managed to pass Angulimala's shield and armour. The Buddha's words, however, pierced his psychological defences. Angulimala was close to tears. The Buddha had struck a chord. Angulimala would dearly like to stop being a bandit. It is not a very happy role. On the other hand, once you have got an identity it seems very difficult to give it up.

'If I stop being a bandit, people will kill me.'

The Buddha understood Angulimala's dilemma. He did his best to help. Angulimala became a monk. The monk's status and robe offer some protection. The Buddha interceded with the king of the country and the latter agreed that as long as Angulimala remained a harmless monk, he would not be hunted down, though on a later occasion a group of people who had suffered through Angulimala's earlier activities did catch him and beat him to within an inch of his life. Nonetheless, Angulimala did achieve inner peace through stopping. He broke the hold of 'being a bandit' upon his behaviour.

In Buddhism, it is this stopping which constitutes 'conversion'. Conversion does not, in Buddhism, mean the intellectual acceptance of a set of beliefs. Conversion occurs when a person deeply sees the state of their life and decides to do something about it. This means seeing how they have been acting in a programmed way and stopping this conditioning from continuing to dominate them. This does not mean that the old conditioning disappears from the person's mind immediately. An enlightened person is not free from conditioning. They are alert to conditioning. I am sure the Angulimala continued to feel impulses to harm for many months and years after his encounter with the Buddha. Fear will have risen up in him powerfully on many occasions. He had seen, however, that immediately after such an arising, there is a gap. There is a point where we have to decide to act or not act on the impulse that has arisen. This gap is the chink through which new light may shine. It is the doorway to enlightenment.

There is a famous story about a Zen Master who is approached by a samurai. The soldier says, 'Your ideas are all nonsense. What is all this about heaven and hell, for instance?' We may guess that the soldier was really frightened that he himself would go to hell for all the things he had done.

The monk affected to look at him with disdain, 'Look at you. Call yourself a soldier. You are a disgrace.'

The samurai's anger surges up and his hand goes to his sword. As he begins to draw the sword with the intention of killing the monk, the Master's manner changes dramatically. Completely without fear, in a gentle but firm voice, he says, 'Here opens the gate of hell'.

The soldier lets the sword fall back into its scabbard. As it does so, the monk says, 'And here opens the gate of heaven,' and smiles. The soldier understands.

The harm we do flows from our conditioning. Most of it we have done before we really ever realise what is happening. We get carried away. Going along in our not-seeing way, acting like robots, we think we have to do the things we do, even when we know perfectly well that they are harmful. Out of our fears and cravings we build an identity for ourselves. The identity we build may not be so dramatic as that of a bandit or a samurai but it becomes just as coercive. Most people feel trapped in their lives. What is necessary is to stop. When we stop acting like robots, we can see what we are doing and everything can change.

Angulimala and the samurai were both trapped by the identities they had created for themselves. The stories they were living were bad ones. It is not easy to get out of a bad story once we have been typecast. These two stories relate encounters between destructive people and enlightened people. In each story a transformation is brought about in the destructive person. A significant enlightenment occurs. The enlightened people, although in danger, do not panic. They do not panic because they are not concerned about themselves. Their ego is out of the way. They are concerned about the other person. Having the ego out of the way does not mean that they are passive or ineffectual. Quite the contrary, they are both very bold. This illustrates what we mean by having one's fire under control. They had fire and they had stillness. It is this combination that made them effective where nobody else could be. The stillness showed at the crucial point, namely when they were most in danger. This stillness in the enlightened person gave the other person pause. The enlightened person and the destructive person are not fundamentally different in nature. It is just that the destructive person has not realised that it is possible to stop. If they do stop they are enlightened too.

These stories convey very well how we need our fire and how we need to have it under control; how stopping is essential to create the space for insight; and how an enlightened person can sometimes help a person who is out of control to discover their potential for a much more worthwhile life.

Part 5

Path

Finding Direction

The Fourth Noble Truth is *Marga*, the path. When we are lost in the woods and we come across a path we feel such relief. Suddenly we feel hope and confidence again. Now we can start going somewhere. We may not yet know exactly where the path will take us, but we know people have been there before. To be on the path means to start going in a consistent direction. If the Third Truth means saying no to the urge to stray, then the Fourth Truth means saying yes to joining the path. This path is the Middle Path. This Middle Path includes both no and yes. It avoids the extremes. In the extremes we are dominated either by yes alone or by no alone.

The ordinary way of thinking is that yes and no are mutually exclusive. This leads either to a struggle for control or to despair. We were recently discussing the Noble Truths in a Dharma group when one member, I'll call her Anna, shared the following:

A few years ago I suffered from cancer. I had treatment which seemed to have been successful. Recently I reached a place where I sensed the cancer had recurred. The uncertainty that I had been struggling to live with for eighteen months became, for a while, overwhelming and intolerable and was accompanied by feelings of doom and fear. I was fighting to get in control, going to see alternative practitioners and doctors, having a scan. I became totally identified with the fight for life – and stopped living.

Ironically, the scan did not yield any information about the very organ I had been concerned for. It had been a waste of time and resources. I realised that I had sunk into a state of panic, had been chasing my own tail, and all to no avail. No amount of activity on my part was going to change the status quo. I realised that it was not within my power to determine the outcome: not in my hands. With this came a sense of relief and release. It was not, after all, my responsibility to stay alive. I had a feeling of what I describe as spiritual confidence – something like Julian of Norwich's 'All shall be well and all manner of things shall be well.' I felt like I had something that could not be taken away from me. Marvellous.

With hindsight, it is clear to me that it was sheer hubris to imagine that I had or could aspire to mastery of my own fate. The experience reminds me of something a friend said to me early on when I was first diagnosed. She said: 'What have you done to deserve God's favour?' It is true that I have received many blessings.

Saying no to the urge to be unrealistically in control allowed Anna to say a real yes to the life she actually does have.

In another group, we were discussing the state of society, the scale of the social problems we face and the difficulty for a citizen alone to effect meaningful change. Richard came in on the discussion with:

I got burnt out with it. For many years I felt as though it was down to me to put the world right. I went on marches and protests and got involved with many organisations. I felt very angry about capitalism and nuclear bombs and ecology and consumerism. It was as though everywhere I looked every-thing was wrong. I just got overwhelmed. So eventually I stopped. I still send money to a few good causes, but that's it. I am still recovering. It is like a kind of convalescence, getting over the devastating effect of realising that I could not change it all.

Richard too has tried the extremes of yes ('I will control it all') and no ('I can't do anything'). He is now evolving a new, happier life and has once again begun to become involved in projects to improve the world, but this time free from the desperate quality that formerly drove him.

The Buddha was offering a Middle Path which enables us to go on being effective without feeling defeated just because we do not sweep all before us. The Four Noble Truths say, in effect, 'This is what you cannot do anything about and this is what you can do something about.' At one extreme is the idea that 'Because I can do something about some things, it must be possible to do everything about everything.' In the modern world this is a popular fallacy. Having lost their religion, many people feel the responsibility for everything now rests entirely upon them. At the other extreme is the thought that 'Because there are some things I will not be able to do anything about – in this lifetime at least – there is no point in doing anything.' This is also a common apathy that afflicts many. It, too, is related to the loss of religion. People are no longer willing to act on faith that the quality of the action alone will ensure that it contributes to good in the world.

The control fallacy is shaped for us by modern history. Religion in the West has been about relating to a God who was a powerful father figure. God was the creator and controller of the universe. What we have tended to do as modern society has emerged is to replace God by Man. It is not so much that people have stopped believing in the God idea. It is that they have put humankind up as a new God. There is current a kind of humanism that puts people centre stage and expects humankind, either individually or collectively, to solve all problems and right all wrongs. The modern person thus harbours a guilt whenever they are failing to be perfectly happy and successful – which is all the time. In the modern mentality it is not so much that God has disappeared from our consciousness as that God has been internalised and we have become our own God. The self has to be appeased because it is now God

The Buddha taught a path which relies neither upon an external nor an internal all powerful god. In the tradition, it is said that a buddha is 'teacher of gods and people'. This means that it is more important to be enlightened than to be all-powerful. God is a power play. If we see God as outside ourselves, then we ally ourselves with him or her and this makes us the chosen people who have superior status and rights over others. If we see ourselves as gods, then we either fall into dissipative selfishness or we wear ourselves out trying to do the impossible. When we do wear ourselves out we can fall into despair.

The Buddha, therefore, taught, firstly, that affliction is real and noble; secondly, that the feelings that come up in us in response to it are also real and noble; thirdly, that we can capture and harness those feelings – just as one might capture and harness a wild horse; and, fourthly, that by doing so we can enter upon a wholesome, constructive and satisfying way of life. In other words, he taught us, on the one hand, to recognise what we cannot do anything about and stop feeling frustrated about that and to recognise what we can do something about and start doing it.

This means doing something about ourselves. Often this begins with facing our own despair. Anna and Richard both had to go through the despair which arose when they faced the overwhelming scale of what afflicted them. Since different parts of us do not all grow up at the same rate, we may need to go through this birth channel of despair several times in the course of our lives. The Four Noble Truths describe this process. They are not a prescription for escape but for maturity.

There is a need within Dharma practice communities to create time and space for this despair work, as Joanna Macy calls it in her book, *Despair and Personal Power in the Nuclear Age* (1983). If we can understand the Buddha's first talk, then we can see the need for this very clearly. The Buddha was not saying that we should not have such feelings. He was saying that in these very feelings lies the energy which can provide the motive force for the spiritual life, for walking the Noble Path. We should have groups to do this work. We should be willing in our Dharma discussions to share these feelings and to listen deeply to one another. Despair is samudaya. Samudaya is not the cause of suffering. Samudaya is the essential second step of a four-step process which leads to the wholesome life.

It is necessary to take the first step which is to share and recognise how we and others are afflicted. It is necessary to take the second step of sharing and recognising how that makes us feel. These are two essential steps. It is then necessary to take the other two steps. The third step is to see that in these feelings lies the energy we need. We can trust the process of self-transformation as long as we can provide a container for it. We need to hold these feelings securely. This is nirodha. Then we need to take the fourth step which is to say yes to a positive path of living. Actually, if we can do the first three steps, the fourth follows naturally. By the time we have got to the fourth step, if we have done the first three well, we already have the necessary momentum.

The Middle Path, the Eightfold Way, is not the means to eliminate suffering. It is the noble outcome of facing the reality of affliction and working through what then comes up for us in a courageous and authentic way. When we do so, the eight elements of the path described by the Buddha are not means to an end. They are simply a description of our authentic life. The Eightfold Path emerges from the spiritual work described in the first three Truths.

· 20 ·

The Big Story

What story are you living? What kind of story is it? Is it a story that you will feel glad to have lived? Will you, when old, look back down the years without regret? These are important questions. Many people feel as though their lives have not really begun yet. They are waiting for the right conditions to begin. Others feel as though it is all over already. Some feel a sense of purpose, but many feel that their lives are disjointed, inconsequential or seriously compromised.

In each life there is a big story and a little story. The little story is the story of the ego. The other day I was asked: 'What was the little story of Jesus Christ?' I suppose the answer is that he was a carpenter's son who never managed to get himself either a wife or a proper job and finished up being executed for a rather trivial offence. If this were all there were to it, history would not have noticed.

The satisfactions of the ego are real enough, but they are exceedingly transitory. It is nice to be praised, or to meet with success and acclaim, and it is painful to be ridiculed and to meet with failure and frustration. Such vicissitudes, however, contain nothing lasting or substantial unless we can conserve the energy from them to serve some greater purpose. What is there to carry us through when the little story comes apart? Real satisfaction arises when the little story is integrated into or even subsumed within a big story that is itself worthwhile.

Most people who have made a great contribution in life have gone through a period of disenchantment – a time in the wilderness – during which they not only came to terms with the defeats in their little story, but also found their place in the big one. This conversion in the wilderness, whereby a little life comes out of its individual backwater and enters the mainstream of the big river, is what is meant by enlightenment. By this step, the little ego is overcome.

The circumstances of our birth affect our story deeply. The Buddha was driven by the fact that his mother died when he was seven days old. If this had remained a little story he might simply have felt sorry for himself. He would have grown up and sought solace here and there and nothing very consequential would have come of it. He would probably have become a rather depressed old man who took out his frustrations on those around him while secretly regretting that he had not had the courage to throw over the traces.

As it was, he went out in search of the answer to a fundamental life problem – the meaning of suffering – not just for himself, but for all humankind. He found a solution and spent his life in service to the cause of bringing this message of hope to others. In the process he set in motion a great story – the story of the tradition we call Buddhism – which has given meaning to millions of other people's lives and provided a vehicle for untold good in the world.

A person who has integrated their life into the big story may come to be regarded as a great being and, in retrospect, people then think it was all fore-ordained. This is how we sell ourselves short. We think that our own lives are not so great. Whether our lives amount to anything or not however, depends upon whether we find the courage to put them in the service of a big story and whether the big story we choose is a wholesome one.

Among big stories some are wholesome and some are not. It is likely that, if we do not deliberately give ourselves to a wholesome story, we will get caught up in an unwholesome one. In my own case, I was born shortly after the last world war. The post-war period has been a time in which there has been a great growth in psychological research and understanding in the western world. The original impetus for this research was the question that was left in people's minds after the war: why did ordinary German citizens, not very different from English, French or American ones, participate in the holocaust? Could it happen again? Of course, we now know that the answer is definitely in the affirmative. Genocide has not been uncommon in the post-war period.

Having been born into the generation of hope following the world's largest war, I grew up participating in the idea that, there having been two world wars, a third was a distinct possibility. With the advent of nuclear weapons it is apparent that a third world war would be catastrophically destructive. It would take a very long time for the planet to recover, if indeed it did. There has been a big story running during my lifetime and this big story is about the prevention of war and the survival of the human race.

In the last few decades this story has taken on an added twist. This is summed up in the word ecology. It has become increasingly clear that the threat to humankind is not just from war. It is also from pollution and ecological damage. We are using the planet up at more than replacement rate. War and famine hover over us, just as they have done throughout human history. The difference is that now there is nowhere else to go and, as a result of technological 'advance', the stakes are much higher.

A big story brings a big task. The great work requires something of all of us. If we neglect this, then we remain trapped in our little stories. Modern society tends to operate in ways that isolate us in our littleness. We are encouraged to be consumers and economic units. We are assailed by advertising which carries the constant message that individual indulgence is all that matters. All this serves to weaken our spirit and put our world at risk. As our society becomes more and more spiritually impoverished, it is like a forest drying out in the heat of summer. The danger of a forest fire grows. Accustomed to getting our whims fulfilled, untrained in containing our fire, we too become vulnerable to the kind of social conflagration that has consumed Yugoslavia, brought misery to Northern Ireland and destroyed Chechnya.

The Buddha offered his followers the opportunity to become part of a big story. This is the story of how afflictions are to be met with a noble response so that people may feel complete, satisfied that they have lived a full and enlightened life. It is the story of how the energies within us, that can sometimes seem so destructive, are to be transformed into the driving power for the

salvation of the world. It is a great story, not a trivial one. It is
not just the story of one individual. It is also the story of the
creation of a community of people who live by a higher calling
and it is, therefore, also the story of a home-coming: of people
returning to their spiritual roots, their 'original nature'.

In psychotherapy, people are often struggling to find a place
for themselves in a meaningful story, or trying to pick up the
pieces of a story that came undone. It is not true, however, that
one story is just as good as another. There is a serious danger in
a complex society like our own that the quest for democracy
and equality leads to a kind of moral relativism which is
destructive of society, families, groups and individuals alike. If
we believe that all stories are as good as one another, then no
story can be important. If the story we are living is not
important, then our life will peter into apathy and we will be
defenceless against tyranny and oppression.[1]

There will always be bad big stories waiting to sweep us
away. Indeed, we are already involved in them. By being
consumer citizens we collude with all manner of ill: factory
farming, armaments production, environmental damage, wars
to protect oil supplies, third world debt, to name but a few. It is
important to do better than this, to find a more noble story.

The Buddha enabled many people to see possibilities for their
lives that they had not perceived before they met him. That is
the function of a sage. He was able to speak the other person's
language and to see their life in terms of the bigger picture –
how new meaning could be injected into the person's little story
so that it began to serve the great story of peace and compassion
in the world. He was an inspirer.[2]

Being part of the big story is what is meant by being on a
path or way. The Fourth Noble Truth is the Truth of the path.
The big story, the story of the spreading of peace and harmony
in the world, of constructive and spirited response to obstacles
encountered, and of harmony and co-operation, is what he
invites us to take refuge in. Without such a path, we are unable
to rise to the needs of our time. With it, we can become the
kind of people whose lives become consequential in a great
variety of wholesome ways.

The Middle Way – the mainsteam – emerges directly from the

practice of the first three Noble Truths. The four together constitute one whole. There is adversity. Recognising adversity we feel our passion rise. Protecting our passion from the wind of ego-centred concern we can turn it to the service of good in the world. That service constitutes the path. The path is described from eight perspectives. We will now look at each in turn.

21

Right View

The Buddha would say: 'All views are wrong views,'[1] by which he meant to warn us about how dangerously opinions can hinder the spiritual path. If I am attached to an opinion, then it inevitably gets in the way of clear perception, both of objective and subject phenomena alike.[2] He wanted his followers to have the kind of steady mind that can cope with a crisis and impart strength to others when it is needed.

If all views are wrong views, what about the Buddha himself? Did he not have views? Certainly he did. But he was also capable of that inner stillness that makes fresh perception possible. Stillness enables innocence and experience to merge. This is a practical not a philosophical matter. It is not a matter of definition of words. I think the point that the Buddha is making is that what he is offering is something to do rather than something to spend a long time thinking about. He is saying 'Don't spend ages philosophising. Try it and see.' We should not elevate his statements into absolutes. It is absolutes that he is preaching against. All his teaching is practical advice.

We all know how dangerous views and opinions can be. People come to blows over them. Co-operation between people breaks down over them. The human animal is notable for its skill in communication, but also for its skill in dispute and hostility. It is doubtful whether there is any view that one could hold which would not carry this danger of setting one into conflict with others. The Buddha was acutely aware of the inflammatory potential of clashes of opinion.

The sayings of the Buddha are recorded in five lengthy collections called the *Sutras*. At the very beginning of this huge collection of writings is the Sutra called Brahma's Net. This begins with a description of two wandering holy men, teacher and disciple, walking along the road some distance behind the Buddha and his companions. The teacher and disciple are arguing about the merits and defects of the Buddha's teaching. The Buddha's own disciples hear this argument and start talking about it. The Buddha overhears them and he says: 'If anyone should speak in disparagement of me or of my teaching or of our community, please do not be angry, resentful or upset by it. To become upset in that way would only be a hindrance to you. For if when others criticise me you become angry or upset, you will be unable to judge clearly whether what they are saying is true or false.'

This very practical declaration summarises the Buddha's teaching on views. Getting upset and taking what has been said personally causes unnecessary suffering and clouds the mind. It is a case of the fire being caught by the ego wind. The Buddha believes in and is completely behind the teaching he gives. He is not arguing that one view is as good as another. Yet he is also open to hear what the other person has to say, to receive criticism and to consider what is right and wrong dispassionately.

As the *Zenrin*,[3] a classic collection of Buddhist wisdom, says

> *Be one who sleeps well.*
> *Undisturbed by 'true or false'.*

The mind which is free and unburdened is naturally inquiring. To be free and unburdened does not mean a restriction of activity so much as a lightness in regard to it. An enlightened person thinks about the future sometimes, but does not become oppressed by a sense of what must be achieved or of what could happen. An enlightened person thinks of the past sometimes, but does not become weighed down by agonising over what has 'gone wrong'. They do not hang onto past hurts. An enlightened person thinks about the present state of things sometimes, but they do not become burdened by what they see.[4]

It is important, therefore, not to invest our ego in our views, however strong our conviction may be. Even Buddhist views are subject to the danger of becoming the justification for intoler-

ance and conflict. As a result of the Buddha giving this teaching
on views such prominence, the Buddhist record on tolerance
has actually been remarkably good over the centuries, but it is
by no means perfect. All systems of thought have their dangers,
even the most benign.

Opinionatedness is very close to what most people mean by
ego. It is attachment to opinions that leads to the fire of our
passion getting out of control, just as much as or even more
than attachment to the pleasures of the senses.

What then is Right View? Outwardly, Right View is total
attention. Inwardly, it is stillness. The word 'right' here means
wholehearted. Right View is not an opinion, it is willingness to
look listen and flow. The path begins with deep listening and
deep seeing.

Such listening and seeing, however, is not devoid of intelli-
gence. Innocence is not ignorance. The Buddha was a practical
person. He adapted his teaching to the mentality and experience
of each person he met, while still staying true to the bigger story
of which we are all a part. If a priest of another religion came
to see him he did not say 'Give up your faith and accept mine,'
but rather found ways of injecting greater meaning into the
practice which the person already followed. Wisdom was set
within empathy. Thus, Right View avoids both relativism, at
one extreme. and dogmatism at the other.

Getting caught in point-scoring is simply a waste of energy. It
is like getting burned by the very fire which could have cooked
your dinner or, as the Buddha put it on another occasion, like
picking up a snake by the tail and getting bitten.[5] There are safe
ways to handle fires and snakes, but they need to be learned.

If we approach life with an open yet dedicated mind, what do
we experience? We experience the Noble Truths. We experience
the suffering that is in the world in all its particular manifesta-
tions. This is how the fire begins and this is why Right View is
the first step. The Eightfold Path is an eight-step training in fire
management. Right View enables us to see and deeply feel the
suffering in the world, to notice our heartfelt response, to see
the possibility for harnessing and directing that response. You
have to be alert when you are playing with fire.

To make a useful fire, we begin by creating a sheltered

fireplace, and bringing together fuel and a spark. All of these initial steps fall within Right View. Our inner life must be sheltered from the ego wind. The inflammable material within us must be managed correctly. The spark is provided by our openness to the suffering in the world. Perceiving dukkha, both within us and around us, is the spark that lights the fire of our spirit. And there is no shortage of sparks.

None of us knows what is going to happen next. Later today I might discover that one of my children had had a terrible accident, or you might discover a lump in your body which indicated that you have cancer, or a war might break out in some part of the world, killing thousands of innocent people. Things like this are happening all the time. On the one hand we live in a beautiful paradise. We inhabit this exquisite blue planet with all manner of quite miraculous wonders all around us. On the one hand . . . on the other hand . . . Life is like that.

We can be ambushed. We are going along happily enough perhaps, when suddenly our world is turned upside down. The moment when three large men have jumped on you in a back alleyway is not the time to start learning self-defence. It is much better to have trained oneself to the point where one can handle the situation without a second thought. The path which the Buddha advocated increases our capacity to cope with life's ambushes.

Actually, just about anything can be an ambush. The more aware we become of our lives, the more we realise just how blind we have been. Every time that greed or hate gets the better of us, we have suffered another injury to our spirit. So, in practical terms, Right View is about resolving to do something about the compulsiveness in our lives in all the thousand and one ways that it pops up in the course of an ordinary day. If we work at this, then when the big ambushes arrive we will be prepared.

What we can be sure of is that they will indeed arrive. Disease, decay and death will come. Disappointment, failure and loss may seem to be things that we might be cunning enough to circumvent, but if we think so, then we are deceiving ourselves. Nobody gets away unscathed in these respects. Often clients in therapy nowadays believe that their lives have been irremediably damaged by their having been abused in some way in the past. However, everybody gets abused in one way or another. To say this is not to diminish the experience, but to emphasise the universal aspect. The suffering in the world is not something for us each to solve on our own. It is of concern to us all. It is by reaching out to one another that we can respond to our collective pain in a noble and constructive way.

None of this is hidden. We all know full well that death will come. We are all exposed to transiency. It is clear as daylight. Yet all too often we live our lives pretending it will not happen to us. We try to find a refuge in self-deception and search for security. We turn even religion into a bulwark against reality, when its only real function is to help us to live authentically.

> Nothing is hidden;
> It has always been clear as day.

> For divine wisdom: look at the old pine tree;
> For eternal truth: listen to the birds sing.

> Seeking the mind: there is no place to look;
> Can you see the footprints of flying birds?

> Above, not a single tile to shelter under;
> Below, not a morsel of ground for support

The *Zenrin* is full of such good advice. Right View is to have this kind of freedom that looks for nothing in the way of support or shelter from the existential reality of our lives. When we have the courage to live life as it is, no longer running away, well grounded, then we experience a profound relaxation in our heart. We put down the burden and no longer have to live defensively.

> In life, seek no heaven;
> In death, fear no hell.

> Enter the woods without disturbing a blade of grass;
> Enter the water without making waves.

Meet the enlightened one on the street;
Do not greet him with words nor silence.

Just laugh and laugh –
In the forest, so many fallen leaves.

For so long, like a bird in a cage;
Now fly free like a cloud in the blue sky.

Hold the hoe with empty hands;
Ride the ox by standing on your own feet.

These verses point to an innocence of mind that is yet fully mature. The enlightened person is mature enough to enjoy life as it is and by doing so liberates the creative fire within. The ox is an age old symbol for the wildness in us that is also the basis for our spiritual life. If we can catch and tame the ox, we will be in command of our power.[6]

22

Right Thought

What should we think? What should we not think? The Buddha was very clear about this.

> 'He abused me, he beat me, he defeated me, he robbed me.'
> In those who harbour such thoughts hatred is not appeased.
> 'He abused me, he beat me, he defeated me, he robbed me.'
> In those who do not harbour such thoughts hatred is appeased. Hatreds never cease through hatred in this world; through love alone they cease. This is an eternal law.[1]

Right Thought follows directly from Right View. If we view others as our enemy, then we will think harmful thoughts. We will plot and scheme against them. Our secret life will be full of terrible imaginings. Just as there is a radiant, innocent, creative child in each of us, so there is also a murderous, hateful, greedy, tyrannical child as well.

It is important to recognise both sides of our nature and not expect to be too good. The novelist Fay Weldon suffered from nightmares as a child and until well into her twenties. Later she came to the conclusion that: 'Nightmares happen, I now believe, to people who think they are good, and fail to acknowledge their own dreadfulness. Children are always the heroes of their own lives: as one grows older one comes to realise one is the villain too.' One night when on holiday, she put her children in a room of a hotel that she was frightened to sleep in herself because it reminded her of her nightmare. 'I am not proud of it. Mothers should not behave like this. They should give up their lives and sanity for their children. I knew the better way, but chose the worse. I was not a good person.' After this incident, she never had the nightmare again. What had changed was that she admitted her 'dark side' into her life.[2]

Along with the light there will always be shadow. This is the inner aspect of the fact that along with bliss there will always be dukkha in the world. The introspective side of the First Noble Truth is to see clearly just how much negativity there is within us. There may be rage and grasping hidden behind the exterior that we present to public view. In civilised people this hidden rage mostly creeps out in sly criticism and subtle angling for advantage rather than in bloody feuds. It is always waiting in ambush, always on the look out for opportunities to create greater mayhem. After all, Bosnia was a civilised country full of civilized people, not so very different from ourselves and so was the pre-war Germany that put the Nazis into power.

When we are able to see our own negativity clearly we will be less complacent and we will not stand in judgement over others. We will know that we too have all the seeds in us to be every possible kind of saint or sinner. We are not made of different stuff from the people we might choose to scorn. To be proud of ourselves while devaluing others is simply self-deception. If we have some special talent or some particular virtue, then we have it for a purpose, which is to benefit the world. If we see it as a platform from which inwardly to assert our superiority, we defeat our real purpose immediately.

Dealing with affliction is only possible if we can get some control over our thoughts, but this does not mean that our thoughts should always be good ones. Horrible thoughts also arise. This is samudaya. The shadow must be admitted. If we can live with the devil in us as well as the angel we will be a lot healthier. The Buddhist way is not necessarily always nice.

When we first adopt this practice, our thoughts include a lot of wrathful energy. We feel angry about the injustices in the world. We think we would like to destroy the torturers with their own instruments – rather as King Ashoka, on first learning about the Buddhist principles of non-oppressive government, is reputed to have boiled the state torturer in his own glue pot![3] Hatred, however, does not cease with hatred. We have to husband the fire in such a way that it becomes love rather than hate. This is achieved by seeing deeply into the hearts of others.

This is what is required of one who would be a therapist for the world.

The path described in the Four Noble Truths is that of transformation. The horrible thoughts can be harnessed, too. In fact, they are the makings of the inner fire that becomes our enlightened nature. The Chinese Dhyana Master Yuan Miao (1238–95) taught that it was essential to discover 'the mind of great anger', 'the mind of great ferocity' and 'the mind of great doubt' within ourselves and to cultivate these qualities in the service of our quest for enlightenment.[4]

When a person who is following this path conscientiously feels anger or disappointment or greed or any such impulse rising up, they do not immediately start to look for someone or something outside themselves to blame. They smile to themselves and think, 'Ah, now the energy is rising,' and they welcome it. For spiritual training this is very profitable, provided that we can keep our nerve. Then we can see that the person who insulted us or cheated us has actually done us a favour. The habit of angry thought, when seen clearly, becomes a source of fire for our furnace.

Now, of course, it is only possible to think like this if following the path of spiritual training or enlightenment is more important to us than short-term personal advantage. If we are just interested in selfishness, we are soon out of control and reduced to a thoroughly ignoble way of being.

Spirituality requires a longer view. Or we may say it requires us to attend to a different dimension of the situation in hand. We might talk loosely about there being a horizontal and a vertical dimension to life. The horizontal dimension is the mundane aspect. It is concerned with the preoccupations of money, relationships, work, personal security, advancement and danger. It is about 'having'. The vertical dimension is all about 'being'. The vertical dimension is the province of spirituality and meaningfulness. Our modern society is all about 'having'. We even call it the consumer society. The Buddha's renunciation was a dramatic enactment of the shift from 'having' to 'being'. He simply gave up everything material and adopted the home-less life. When we give up 'having', then we put ourselves in a position of having nothing to defend and so the basis for

attachment to negative states of mind is cut away.[5] Simply being
is what Buddhism is about. When we simply are, then we find
that we are not cut off from the existence of everything. The
enlightenment experience is an experience of being one with
everything.

The thought of enlightenment, or the thought of the vertical
dimension, or the higher purpose of life, or whatever other
name one wishes to give to it, is, therefore, a supremely
important thought. It is the thought which enables us to focus
on being rather than having, on the quality of our moment by
moment living rather than on the quantity of what we are
getting. This thought is important enough in Buddhism to have
a name. It is called *bodhichitta*. In the Mahayana schools of
Buddhism, the bodhichitta is regarded as of supreme importance. It is by keeping the thought of higher purpose in mind
that we are able to let go of all the trivia that otherwise would
constantly lead to greed, hate and delusion in our everyday
lives.

The bodhichitta may also be called 'the thought of great
compassion'. It is the essence of the transformation in human
mentality which the Buddha was working for. The transformed
human being is called a bodhisattva. In Buddhist mythology
there is an ideal buddha and an ideal bodhisattva. These ideals
exist to help us aspire to a better life and to find the vertical
dimension of existence. In Buddhist iconography, the ideal
buddha is called Amida and the ideal bodhisattva is called Quan
Yin.[6] Amida means 'measureless'. This draws our attention to
the fact that the vertical or spiritual dimension is unconditional.
When we think of it, we are not thinking about things that we
can calculate. When we give a gift with an ordinary mind, some
calculation goes on. We measure out our generosity. When we
give a gift with an enlightened mind there is no calculation. We
just give, without any ulterior motive.

In Buddhism we say that this latter kind of giving is 'empty'.
This leads to many seemingly puzzling statements in Buddhist
writings which are not really as odd as they first seem. We read
of 'no mind' and 'the thought of no thought' and so on. Actually
this is all quite close to common usage which is a practical and
not a literal use of language. When we say that the best kind of

friend is 'one who would help you without a thought', we do not mean that they literally would not think. We mean that they would act in our interests without reservation. They would not count the cost to themselves. There would be no self in their decision.

The name Quan Yin means 'hearer of the cries', and it refers to a heart moved to compassion. She 'regards all beings with a compassionate eye'.[7] Quan Yin always hears the cry in the heart. When a person acts badly, it is because there is a cry of pain in their heart. Quan Yin hears this cry. She is thus able to regard everybody with deep empathy because she has this ability to see deeply. This is what is required of a helper. The great American psychologist Carl Rogers coined the term 'unconditional positive regard' for the attitude that a psychotherapist needs to have toward their client.[8] This term, unconditional positive regard, is very close to an amalgam of the names Amida and Quan Yin.

When we recognise, acknowledge and contain our own afflictions and are no longer afraid of the shadows that arise within ourselves, we put ourselves in a position to think well of others and to become useful in the world. Right Thought is the thought that puts the higher purpose at the centre of our existence and does not exclude anything from its orbit.

23

Right Speech

The Buddha did not waste words. His words were well chosen and to the point. They came from his depths. They were sincere and beautiful. They touched people's hearts and moved them to positive action. The speech of a buddha is both a healing and a creative force in the world. Not only that, but it puts the hearer in touch with what is beyond the ordinary world, what is on the vertical dimension. The words of a buddha, although intrinsically beautiful, may therefore sometimes be shocking to the ordinary mind. They challenge its most basic assumptions. They place no value on having, getting, accumulation nor security. They do not laud power and privilege, nor do they carry any assumption that the goal is the pursuit of pleasures. If we consider our own speech in this light, we may well see that it is very different from that of a buddha.

Buddha saw the potential of communication. What has come down to us is the example of his life and much of it was spent communicating. He was an exceptionally effective and purposeful communicator. The purpose was to convey the message of peace in the world through peace in the heart. He advocated that we should be reconcilers of those at variance, encouragers of those at one, rejoicing in peace, loving it, delighting in it, speakers of words that make for peace.[1] The Buddha put his passion into bringing peace to the world. This was his life and we can continue his life by doing likewise.

He knew that the attainment of such peace requires great courage. It requires courage to change one's ways. In this respect the Buddha was a great therapist. His words gave people the courage to make major changes. Often these changes were not easy. Just as nowadays, parents and relatives were not always enthusiastic about their children leaving home to follow a wandering meditation teacher and more than one would-be disciple had to go on hunger strike to obtain parental permission. In those days, parents had more power than today, extending to adult children as well as minors.

The Buddha taught a lot about Right Speech. There are many instances of people coming to him and being enlightened by a single conversation. People met him, talked with him and then changed their lives. Many of them then went on to inspire others. Thus there was a ripple effect. The Buddha's greatest disciple, Shariputra, became a disciple after hearing another quite inexperienced monk, Assaji, give a very sketchy account of Gautama's teaching.[2] Centuries later the great Zen Master Hui Neng had his first enlightenment experience by hearing a man reading a sutra in the street.[3] Words can have great power.

Many of the people the Buddha enlightened spent very little time with him. Others spent years by his side. It is not that they learned a method whereby to obtain something called enlightenment as though this were a possession one could acquire. If we think of spirituality in this worldly way, we simply bring the sublime down to the level of the mundane. What is required is the reverse: to raise everything mundane to the level of the sublime. When a person is inspired, every situation becomes a stimulus for joy and creativity. When a person is not inspired, even the most elevating circumstances are converted to dross. Cynicism for instance is the cancer of spirituality.

Inspiration is closely associated with aspiration. When we are inspired, we aspire. When we aspire it is much easier for things to inspire us. The two go together. Right Speech is the utterance of inspiration and aspiration. In Buddhism, the utterance of aspiration is called the vow.

Vows are out of fashion in the modern materialistic world because they do not fit into the horizontal dimension. A vow is an unconditional commitment. It goes beyond calculation. It is a statement that 'I will . . .' no matter what the odds against me may be. When we vow something we take it in a total way. A vow is not a prediction of success. Modern people tend to say, 'I will not promise something until I am sure that I can deliver it.' This is a conscientious thought and it is related to a concern for fair dealing. Really it is, however, still part of the conditional, contractual, horizontal way of thinking. It also, in western culture, has as its backdrop the fear of punishment. In the Judeo-Christian tradition the wrath of God is to be feared. If you promise something to God and you do not deliver, he will punish you. So the thought arises, 'better not promise in the first place.' This 'better not', however, tends to make for a spiritually limp existence. It is like shooting oneself in the foot.

In Buddhism, the meaning of vows is different because the context is different. In the first place, there is no God. In the second place, consequences will follow from your actions whether you promised or not. Whether you promised to stop smoking or did not promise to, the chance of contracting cancer is still the same. The chance of getting cancer is related to whether you do or do not smoke, not to whether you do or do not promise. The same is true with ethical commitments. Actions have consequences. If you steal, you harm yourself and others, whether or not you had previously promised to be honest.

Thirdly, a vow, in the Buddhist sense, is not quite the same thing as a promise. I promise to pay you back the money you gave me is really part of a contractual culture which belongs to the horizontal dimension. In the language of Jesus, we might say that it belongs to Caesar. A vow is something different. Let me give an example. A person lives in a country that has been overrun by an enemy. There are soldiers in the street. The people are everywhere oppressed. The person feels the injustice of the situation very deeply. This depth of feeling is expressed in a vow: 'I will free our land of these invaders.' This is a vow because it is made unconditionally. As a matter of fact, the person does not know whether it is possible to fulfil the vow. The enemy may be too strong. That, however, is not the point. A vow is not conditional upon possibility. A vow comes from depth of feeling. A vow connects our little life to a big story.

It becomes a central organising force. It sets a person on a path. All effort is directed toward its accomplishment. The person's sense of identity changes. In this case, he has become a freedom-fighter. The quality of even the ordinary things of life changes. He is constantly aware of the way in which every action does or does not contribute to the cause. He is in the grip of a powerful inspiration. People who are inspired in this way, like Gandhi, for instance, often achieve seeming miracles. Their energy all flows one way. The vow has an organising effect upon character.

The difference between a person who lives by vow and a person who does not is like the difference between a piece of ordinary iron and a magnet. In the ordinary piece of iron, the atoms are all higgledy-piggledy so their individual forces cancel each other out. The overall effect is neutral. This is like the ordinary person who drifts about dissipating their energy on things that arise by chance. In the magnet, all the atoms are aligned so that their forces reinforce one another. The overall effect is to create a powerful force field that draws in other pieces of iron and magnetises them too. A person who lives by vow has a magnetised life. The Buddha was a great magnet. Many of the most talented people of his day went to see him and this is one reason why we still, twenty five centuries later, feel his effect upon the world.

A person who has vowed to free his country may meet with many setbacks. It will not be plain sailing. He or she may be defeated many times. They may sometimes fall into despair. Sometimes there will be triumphs. Much of the time it will be a long hard slog. Intense relationships will form from which will come the most intense emotions. It will not be secure, but it will be intense. It will not be an easy life. The person will not be able to count on success, and will have to be willing to sacrifice anything in the cause. They will, by making such a vow, have relinquished all the things that ordinary people cling to. Although they will have, in one sense, lost everything, they will, in a more important sense, have found the meaning of their life. Jean Paul Sartre wrote, reflecting upon his time working in the French Resistance during the war, 'it was when we were most oppressed that we were most free.' The vow, in one sense, coerces every aspect of life yet, in a more important sense, it liberates. The more important sense is that it liberates a person from attachment to trivia. If a fighter in the French Resistance were required to give up her house she would do so without calculation of personal advantage, because it served the cause.

The vow gives life coherence and meaning and frees the person to do things they would never contemplate in more settled times. The vow unsettles our old life.

The epitome of Buddhist speech, therefore, is the vow. There is a sense in which the Buddhist is a kind of freedom fighter. When we look around, we see that our land is indeed overrun by a powerful enemy. The soldiers of the enemy are greed, hate and delusion. When we are constantly being pushed around by greed, hate and delusion, we are everywhere oppressed and our lives remain on the flat horizontal plane. In this circumstance we may put our energy into distracting ourselves from the inauthenticity of our existence: a depressing prospect. Or, we may strike out for liberation.

The Buddha inspired people to become freedom fighters. He used the military metaphor a good deal. He had been brought up to be a warrior. He saw that the true victory was to conquer oneself rather than to conquer others.[4]

The Buddha also used the metaphor of creating a land which was free from the enemy: a Pure Land. When the Buddha talked about Amida,[5] he told a story, like a fairy story, of how, long long ago, Amida had formerly been a king called Dharmakara.[6] At that time, a buddha appeared in the world. This buddha was called Lokeshvararaja. Dharmakara immediately gave up his throne and went to meet this Buddha. He was so impressed by what he saw that he exclaimed, 'I announce that the aspiration of highest enlightenment has awakened in me. Please tell me what I should do to establish a pure land.' Lokeshvararaja said: 'You must already know what to do.' Dharmakara was confused and asked again for instruction. Lokeshvararaja then said: 'There is no vow which cannot be fulfilled!' And he went on to describe the perfection of the world perceived by a buddha. Dharmakara was inspired to adopt the Noble Path without reservation. He then expressed his inspiration by proclaiming a list of forty-eight vows and a verse which ends, 'If these vows are to be fulfilled, let the universe shake and the devas send down cascades of heavenly flowers!' And according to the story this is what happened and Dharmakara in due course became Amida Buddha. Dharmakara was enlightened by his own words just as much as by those of his teacher. The Buddha's words point us toward what we already know and give us the inspiration to do something about it.

The attention of ordinary people is generally upon endpoints. Ananda, who was listening to this story, naturally wanted to know whether Dharmakara did become enlightened and establish a pure land. The story, however, takes place in mythical time and so is intended to be applicable to all people at all times. When the Buddha says, 'Yes, Dharmakara fulfilled his vow,' he means that we can fulfil our vows. Knowing that 'There is no vow which cannot be fulfilled' is inspiring. The aspect of the story which is of immediate relevance to us is that it suggests that we must find the vow in ourselves. Dharmakara found his vow. We must find our own and speak it out just as he did.

The idea here is that there is a vow already buried deep within each of us, a 'primal vow' which is just crying for an opportunity to come out. When Dharmakara saw the Buddha, he cried out his vow. This was not really a case of a pupil being given instruction which he then follows and so achieves something. It was a case of a person, Dharmakara, who had a pent up longing to be all that he could be, coming in contact with another person, Lokeshvararaja, who inspired him to get on with the task he already knew was right and necessary.

Enlightenment is not the end point. Enlightenment is the beginning. Dharmakara became fully alive as soon as he saw what needed doing. His speaking out his vow was his declaration of his new life. Similarly, Kondañña cried out with joy. Actually, the pure land of bliss exists as soon as a person starts to let their energy flow in this way.[7] What could be more blissful than knowing one is on the right path?

The point at which we get in touch with our own primal vow, our own deepest longing, and dare to believe that it is possible to live it, and make this the open declaration of our lives, is the turning point. That is when we shift from the horizontal to the vertical dimension. That is enlightenment. After that one is a freedom fighter. In this new life there are many ups and downs. That is what having a vertical dimension is all about. This is a passionate path: 'impassioned for peace' said the Buddha.

· 24 ·

Right Action

The enlightening effect of contact with a buddha is due to the fact that the way such a person is in itself demonstrates that we too can be all that we have the potential to be. This does not mean that a buddha goes round doing spectacular things all the time in a showy sort of way. A buddha simply is what he or she is. They are not pretentious. They simply live out their truth unabashedly. They do not expect life to be easy, particularly. They do not expect praise all the time. There *is* hardship and affliction. These afflictions bring up many feelings. That is natural. We do not have to be overwhelmed, however. These invasions can be contained by the primal vow.[1] They put fire in our belly. When we are guided by our aspiration to the highest purpose, every situation, good or ill, becomes more fuel for the fire.

A meaningful life has this quality of working with whatever is to hand. It is not a matter of creating a particular state of affairs. An enlightened person might live in riches or in poverty, in a time of peace or a time of war. Nowadays, most of us live in what would have seemed extreme riches to our ancestors. Materially society progresses, but spiritually, the challenge is still the same.

Right Action begins with self-restraint. This seems paradoxical to the person caught on the horizontal dimension. In the flat world, more means better. The more choice we have, the happier we think we will be. The more we get, the more pleased we think we will be. That is horizontal thinking. The spiritual path begins with giving some things up. On the vertical dimension, most of the things the flat-landers cherish seem like unnecessary baggage. How can one rise to the heights while carrying so much ballast?

When a person becomes a Buddhist they make certain declarations. These are generally in the form of 'Refuges' and 'Precepts'. Different schools of Buddhism word them somewhat differently from one another but the essential meaning is much the same throughout the Buddhist world. The Three Refuges are the first vow. They are a declaration that from now on one will take refuge in the Buddha, the Dharma and the Sangha. Buddha here means both the historical Buddha and the buddha nature in oneself and all beings. Dharma means both the historically given teachings and the truth as it manifests in everything all the time. Sangha means both the great teachers of the past who are our spiritual ancestors and the community of all people in the present time who are following the Middle Way. By implication, this means that one will not take refuge in money, security, status and all the other things that constitute the worldly way. Taking refuge therefore, effects one's shift from what we have been calling a horizontal life to a vertical one. It means waking up and getting onto one's feet. The Precepts are a summary of the moral code taught by the Buddha. Taking Refuge is to express one's primal vow. Taking Precepts is to say 'And this is going to make a difference to my life.'

The ethics of Buddhism are extensive. The Buddha taught at great length about what we should and should not do. None of this is new to us. It is simply important for it to be said and acted on. We already know that hurting people is not good. We already know that dishonesty and theft are not good. We know that improper sexual relations lead to no end of trouble. We know that consuming intoxicants does us no good and opens the door to behaviour we later regret. Right action means taking our life in hand.

Lokeshvararaja said to Dharmakara: 'You must already know what to do. Even though this was true, Dharmakara still found it inspiring to hear it said. We need inspiration to show us what is possible. We know intuitively what is right, but we need help to actualise what we know or it just remains an unrealised potential.

Right Action is the fourth step of the Eightfold Path. It does not stand alone. Morality should not be taken out of its spiritual context. When we live from our vow, moral action is a natural corollary. Morality that is not rooted in right view, right thought and right speech, however, can rapidly degenerate into repression.

The Buddha's standard is simple and direct: Cease from harm; do only good; do good for others. Do not kill. Do not create the cause for others to kill. Do not collude in killings, either of people or of other sentient beings. Do everything possible to avert war. Do not support the meat trade. Do not take what should belong to others. Share. Use what you have for the good of the world. Be hospitable. Respect others. Do not engage in sexual relations without love and commitment. Be responsible in bringing new life into the world. Encourage one another in what is good. Speak truthfully. Speak well of others and not of their faults. Avoid all drugs and alcohol. Treat the world and all its creatures with loving care. Live simply and perform actions that benefit individuals, families, society and the natural world.

He lived what he taught. The Diamond Sutra is a discourse on profound wisdom. It may be considered one of the Buddha's most advanced teachings. The text deals with the attitude of mind of the bodhisattva who saves all sentient beings while not himself considering that he is doing anything special or out of the ordinary. The text begins like this:

Thus have I heard. Once Buddha was staying at Anathapindika's Park near Shravasti along with about 1250 monks. One day, at the time for breaking fast, the Blessed One put on his robe, took his bowl, and made his way into the great town of Shravasti to beg for his food. In the city he begged from door to door according to rule. This done, he returned to his place and ate his meal. When he had finished, he put away his robe and his bowl, washed his feet, arranged his seat and sat down.

Then his disciple Subhuti approaches him and the dialogue unfolds. We might think that this paragraph is insignificant: mere scene setting. However, what it demonstrates is that the Buddha himself lived in exactly the same simple way as all his nuns and monks. He was a beggar.

Right Action begins, therefore, with a radical simplification of life brought about by applying some basic moral precepts. This gives life a new vigor. Initially, this simplification frees up a vast amount of energy. If all that happens, however, is that a person then remains within a straitjacket of rules without significant outlet for the energy, the whole spiritual enterprise may turn sour.

Enlightenment is inspiration. Inspiration needs expression. Otherwise it is like breathing in without breathing out. The Buddha was a charismatic teacher who radiated a powerful field of energy. Those who start to be carried along by this energy, need to apply it for the good of the world. It is a path and a path goes somewhere. The bodhisattva – the enlightenment being – has the transformation of the whole world in view. This is not in the sense of an ambition. It is simply that once the energy is liberated it has to be used. It is like the fairy tales in which a genie has been trapped in a bottle for a thousand years. Once the genie is out of the bottle, it is very hard to put it back.

Not only does the bodhisattva need to express their 'passion for peace', but the world needs such people. Enthusiasm is infectious. The spirit of the world must not be allowed to curdle and die. Spirited people are needed to kindle it. We need a corps of inspired people who will work together for the betterment of the world. There is a great work to be done. There are plenty of people who do not know how to handle the hurt inside themselves who are devoting great energy and discipline toward some very destructive purposes in this world. If the effect of human presence on this planet is to be benign rather than malignant there is a great need for even more dedicated people to be working for the cause of great compassion.

If we do not put ourselves forward to become part of the solution, we will remain part of the problem. More, however, is required than simple enthusiasm. It is important to find a place for ourselves in the big story, but it is also important to make sure it is the right big story. There are many big stories around that are cruel, greedy and built on delusions. They will carry us along if we do not find a firmer footing. War, for instance, is a big story. Many people remember the war as 'The best time of my life'. It was the best time because it was a big story that lifted them out of their little self and gave meaning to life. However, it was a terrible story and one we should not wish to repeat. Many people settle for little inconsequential lives precisely because the only big stories they know about are terrible ones. What is needed is for us to demonstrate by our actions that a good big story is possible. Such was the Buddha's mission: that all the energy generated by the affliction that is in the world should be turned to the work of creating a path for the good of the many, for the happiness and well being of all beings.

Right Livelihood

Right Livelihood is not just about how one earns one's money. It is about finding the lifestyle which will further the great work.

Yelui Chu Tsai[1] was a young man of the Khitan race, living in Beijing in the early thirteenth century. This was the time of Genghis Khan's invasion of northern China. Beijing was under siege. Yelui studied Buddhism inside the city and went on an intensive retreat. In 1215 he experienced a breakthrough in his understanding of the Dharma. He felt completely inspired. A few days later the city finally fell to the Mongol armies. Yelui, was rounded up, along with many other talented young people that the Mongols thought might be useful to them, and marched back to Mongolia where he was brought before the Khan.

Yelui was still radiant in the effects of his enlightenment experience. Genghis was struck by the young man's demeanour and even more by the fact that he was unwilling to speak in criticism of or disloyalty to his former Chinese masters, despite being in the presence of the Khan who had just defeated them and who had the power to have him executed. The Khan respected fearlessness and loyalty and decided to take Yelui into his service. Yelui was appointed astrologer to the court. Very rapidly he was promoted to become Genghis' chief advisor.

Yelui, an enlightened Buddhist, was now chief minister to one of the most savage characters of history. In this position he participated in all the affairs of state of the rapidly expanding Mongol empire. He always argued for the long-term view: if you destroy a city it will pay no taxes; if you decimate a country, it will not help you in future wars; if you practise unnecessary oppression, you breed rebellion. There are probably several whole nationalities which owe their continued existence on this planet to Yelui's skill and human-heartedness. Yelui also used his position to protect Confucianism and Taoism. Genghis' empire became one of the first on earth to practise genuine religious toleration and the codes of law that came into effect under Yelui's influence were far in advance of their time. Yelui did not become rich. When he died, he left behind only books, musical instruments and a cabinet of medicines.

So it is not necessary to be a monk to carry out the Buddha's intention, nor should we despair of practising on account of adverse circumstance. In fact, we may surmise that it was facing such adversity that drove Yelui's realisation so deep. If he had lived in a time of peace and ease, would he have had so meaningful a life? Perhaps not. The path to enlightenment begins with facing the reality of affliction.

It is difficult for a person to see the meaning of work unless they perceive the need. In our society things have become so sophisticated that it is often difficult to see the connection between what one does and the good that comes of it. Zen Master Dogen wrote: 'It is an act of charity to build a ferry or a bridge and all forms of industry are charity if they benefit others.'[2] However, it is difficult for many people in modern society to see their work as contributing anything useful or valuable, even when it does. People feel as though they are working simply for the money, for an extrinsic reward. Work, therefore, becomes a utilitarian or selfish necessity rather than an offering. The question of Right Livelihood thus becomes perplexing.[3]

Not only is this true at the level of the individual. On a large scale in our society there is a concern with whether there is enough employment as though employment were something quite divorced from its outcome. There are demands for job creation. Really this is a very strange idea. The truth is that certain things need to be done if people are not to go hungry, if dwellings are to be built and maintained, if the sick are to be cared for and so on. In a simple society, the connections between work and outcome are much easier to see. If a village in the mountains in Vietnam does not have a school, the village people may get together and build one. They cut the bamboo to make the walls themselves. Everybody who is involved can see what they are doing and why it matters. The person sitting in county hall in a modern western city dealing with planning applications and fire regulations, processing advertisements to recruit education department staff, or writing reports, does not generally have the same sense of involvement in something important.

Being divorced from the direct perception of need creates a deadening alienation in the worker. Really this is just another facet of the same Noble Truths that the Buddha described. Unless we have full awareness of the affliction that our work is designed to allay, we have little sense of meaningfulness in our occupation. Right Livelihood is not just a question of doing the right job. It is also a matter of consciousness of what the job really means.

I am involved with a venture called the Amida Trust which seeks to implement Buddhist principles in the contemporary world. Contributing to a debate with other members of the Trust, a friend recently wrote to me:

> One of the many questions I would be happy to discuss is 'mindful livelihood'. Since I am still engaged in the treadmill of work-pay-mortgage and have a completely irrational fear of being unemployable (I sometimes think no one will ever want to employ me because I am 'over' qualified), the question often arises for me of why it is that I do what I do and what should I do with the money that I earn and the time that I have. What is the right balance between what I give to myself and what I give to others (in terms of time, presence and financial assistance)? I have just recently bought a house, but is this a wise 'investment' (not in the sense of 'will it pay off financially', but in the sense 'perhaps I should have (a) given the money away to those who need it more than myself, (b) spent it on an Amida Therapy Training course and changed careers . . . etc)?'

This frank piece of sharing by a very sincere modern Buddhist highlights the difficulty. The modern person so often feels that they are on 'the treadmill of work-pay-mortgage' and that their work serves only to bring in necessary money. The analysis that Karl Marx made to the effect that the modern worker necessarily feels alienated from their work is not so far from the truth. Marx believed that religion served the function of keeping the workers from complaining about this situation. It was perhaps because Marx failed to see that religion has revolutionary potential that his efforts to bring about a social renewal have largely petered out. Historically, it is religious groups, on the whole, that have practised communism and the communalistic ethos is strong in Buddhism.

This question of Right Livelihood has been one of the main motivators of my life. I gave up a career in accountancy, not because I did not think that accountancy is an honourable profession – it can be – but because at the time I was engaged in it, I was, via my employers, busy helping to make a number of armaments manufacturers and meat farmers more efficient, which did not sit easily with me as a pacific vegetarian. So I went and worked for an organisation called Children's Relief International which has since become part of Save the Children Fund. That gave me a taste for social work and I subsequently qualified as a social worker. At that time, Throssel Hole Priory Soto Zen Monastery was just getting off the ground, so I applied for and got a job as a social worker in Northumberland so that I could be close to the monastery.

Initially, when I became a disciple of Dhyana Master Jiyu Kennett Roshi three decades ago, she was part of an order in which there was a married priesthood. There were then, just after she settled in the USA, plans for a community of married ordained Zen practitioners. For a short time they had a centre in north California called Kannon Dell (after Quan Yin, the pre-eminent lay bodhisattva in Buddhist mythology). This community foundered for a time. Roshi's new order moved steadily in the direction of adopting the Chinese rather than the Japanese standard for its priests. Celibacy became the rule, and the venture in an ordained married sangha came to a halt. Although they had changed in their goals, I had not.

I am not alone. There is increasing interest in the west in the creation of intermediate status roles: more committed than an ordinary lay person but not a celibate monastic set up. The Tiep Hien Order of Zen Master Nhat Hanh is just one venture in this direction. The Amida Trust is set up as an essentially lay organisation. I hope that it may wax sufficiently to begin to solve the Right Livelihood problem for an increasing number of people. I have come to the conclusion, over the years, that what is needed is to create a new kind of social environment: one that is organic, cohesive, spiritual and creative. I have always wanted not just to have Right Livelihood myself, but to be involved in creating an environment in which increasing numbers of people could find it themselves in a wide variety of ways. I can see the emergence of the Amida Trust as a continuation of this same driving concern which has gone on throughout my life.

Regarding the dilemma, *what should I do with the money that I earn and the time that I have*, I would simply say, use everything for good purposes. The Buddhist lay person is not expected to give everything away. They are encouraged to use whatever they have for good ends. My wife Caroline and I make our house available. We use our time for things that help. We apply our minds to finding the best ways to advance the great work. We practise Dharma together and with others. We do our best. Often this is far short of perfect, but that is not the point.

As for, *I have just recently bought a house, but is this a wise 'investment'*, to me, the answer to this question depends entirely upon what one then uses the house for. Hospitality is one of the foremost Buddhist virtues. If the great work is to be advanced, there will certainly be a need for houses somewhere in it.

And *the right balance between what I give to myself and what I give to others* – for me, this has become an increasingly false dichotomy as I have become more deeply committed. I do not think in these terms. It does not seem like two different directions to me. Most activities could be said to have something of both in them, but it does not seem to be a useful way of approaching life to think that way. My needs are quite well met. I have faith, most of the time, that I will get by one way or another. I am actively engaged in many ventures. For myself or for others? It is all of a piece. I can see that it may be different if one spends all day doing a job that one does not think is part of the great work. If this is the case then I would say change the job. It might be replied that that is easier said than done, but it is possible. I know. There is also, of course, a gradient, rather than a black and white contrast. Some work contributes more, some less, no doubt. Our task is to move toward the light, not to worry about where we happen to be starting from. These are the ideas that have meant much to me.

I was very grateful for my friend's letter because it prompted me to think about my situation and about the general issues it raises more deeply. We need a transformation in our society and this needs to come from a shift of consciousness. In order to bring this about there will need to be people committed to a new view, a non-alienated and non-alienating approach to social life. We have to evolve a new form of post-industrial society in which what people spend their time doing is meaningful and is experienced as being so.

The idea that market forces will create this situation of their own accord – Adam Smith's 'invisible hand' – is not totally wrong, but it is woefully inadequate. While the socially approved motivations are variants of greed, competition and the delusion of status, the 'neutral' mechanism of market forces will simply go on reproducing these oppressive factors unrestrictedly. A full treatise on Buddhist economics is beyond the scope of this book, but if we are to understand Right Livelihood, we must begin again to experiment with forms of sharing, communalism, hospitality, generosity, and small scale non-alienating organisation. We must create an environment in which we work together toward purposes that matter and that further the emergence of a new kind of civilisation. We must avert the decay of community and the spread of civil strife.

· 26 ·

Right Effort

The sixth step of the Eightfold Path is Right Effort or Right Diligence. You could call it tuning in because what is meant is the effort involved in noticing what is coming up in the mind. The traditional formula is that it is the effort (1) to prevent unwholesome states of mind from arising; (2) to eradicate those that have arisen; (3) to bring about wholesome states not yet arisen; and (4) to sustain wholesome states already arisen. I, in less traditional mode, will say that it is the effort to face obstacles, achieve full awareness of arising feelings and commit ourselves to positive action. In the analogy of fire, Right Effort is the activity of tending the fire once it is underway.

The fire needs attention. It needs a supply of fuel and it needs constant care to ensure both that the fuel gets completely burned up and also that the fire does not get out of hand. Burning the fuel up means that there is no residue of regret from our actions. We do not come away thinking, 'if only I had . . .' Right Effort means intensity. 'You must be as audacious as someone trying to grab the eyebrows of a living tiger or to snatch the whiskers of a flying dragon.'¹ Things come up in us. We should be immediately aware of what has arisen.

The last three steps of the Eightfold Path are closely correlated with the last three Noble Truths. The sixth, Right Effort, is concerned with becoming aware of samudaya. We set ourselves to notice what comes up as it comes up. The seventh, Right Mindfulness, is concerned, as we shall see, with protecting the fire by the art of stopping, nirodha. The eighth step, Right Samadhi, is that subjective experience of the transformed life.

Right effort, in the sense that the Buddha used the term, is the means to the setting up of mindfulness. It means being

observant of everything that arises. The practitioner notices
what comes out of the storehouse of the mind as it emerges into
consciousness. This is the awareness of feelings in the midst of
feelings: the practice of meditation.

It is for this reason that the Zen school, which places such
central emphasis upon meditation, is considered to be the school
of effort or 'self-power'. The Zen practitioner makes great effort
sitting still upon his or her cushion. Zen can be very hard work.
In the practice of Zen meditation – called 'sitting zen' – one sits
very still, in the lotus position, left foot on right thigh and right
foot on left thigh, watching the mind. Whatever arises is noted
and allowed to pass. The practitioner does not budge from the
spot, no matter what comes up. In Theravada Buddhism there
is a similar practice called 'choiceless awareness' and most
schools of Buddhism have something similar. In one sense, this
is very hard work as anyone who has attended an intensive Zen
retreat will testify. On the other hand it is simply a matter of
sitting doing nothing. This is the interesting paradox. The
challenge is to do nothing. We are so programmed to react to
stimuli that not doing so requires the highest degree of self-
mastery.

Right effort is a fine tuning of one's effort in cultivating the
mind. The Buddha uses the analogy of tuning a stringed musical
instument.[2] If the strings are too taut or too slack, it will be
impossible to make good music. If a person is either too idle or
over-zealous, they will not live a truly spiritual life. The too
zealous person is unnecessarily hard on themselves. This is the
extreme of asceticism. The slacker lets their life pass without
having really been there.

Recently I was ill. A particularly unpleasant attack of influ-
enza sent me to my bed. Most of the other members of the
family had already had their turn at falling prey to this malady
and were, by then, on the road to recovery. I became very
drowsy and slept a good deal which was to the good. When I
was awake, my body was very uncomfortable. I took stock of
pains arising in my legs, my arms, the back, the shoulders, the
front of the head, the back of the head, the chest – just about
everywhere, in fact. In this situation there was little to do but
endure. I recognised an important spiritual opportunity, none-

theless. Sickness is a great leveller. While it lasts one is just as incapacitated whether one is the least of creatures or king of the world. 'One fever will quench your pride.'[3] There is no opportunity to pursue any of the schemes that one's ego delights in. There is nothing for it but to be patient.

Patience[4] is one of the characteristics of a bodhisattva. The bodhisattva is somebody with a big mind, a big heart, a lot of capacity to take life in their stride and to reach out to people, both in joyful and in difficult times. Each contact with suffering is an opportunity for increasing our capacity for compassion and understanding. Many feelings come up when we are ill. It is not pleasant. Accepting each 'arising' and not allowing it to get caught by the ego which would sweep us away into self-pity or resentment, requires poise.

Sitting on the meditation cushion is an exercise in expanding one's capacity. We set ourselves to sit still for a time. Quite quickly the mind finds all manner of compelling reasons for us to abandon our seat. These impulses afflict us and we are inclined to struggle with them. It is very easy to become enmeshed in a sequence of thoughts that carries us away into a kind of unconsciousness. The person who has done even a limited amount of such meditation soon comes to recognise the difference between the clear awareness of being in touch with here and now reality on the one hand and the dull opaqueness of a mind lost in thought or struggle on the other. In fact, one is only really aware of the latter on the point of waking up from it. As soon as the mind is entranced in this way, however, the spiritual path has been, at least momentarily, lost.

We sit on our cushion by choice. Illness is not chosen, but the effort required, while lying on the sickbed, is similarly that of simply being there. When the body wants to sleep, sleep. When the body is awake, be awake. Being awake, I notice the arising of pain in some part of my anatomy. I notice what arises in my mind in relation to it. I am not carried away by what arises. All these things are ephemeral. It is not comfortable. It is not the end of the world. It simply is what it is. This is what is meant by effort.

Sometimes we think that simply to be would mean to live effortlessly and you will, indeed, come across descriptions of the enlightened state as effortless. We should be careful not to be trapped by the limitations of language here. Life without effort is a contradiction of terms. The enlightened state is not one of idleness. For a living being, effort is part of being. The finely tuned kind of effort that the Buddha has in mind, however, is a kind of pure awareness. Sometimes it is called 'effortless effort'. It is the effort of drawing our attention to what is there.

We are all conditioned in a million ways by our experience. We do not live naturally. We live according to our programming. The effort needed to live the Eightfold Path is that of applying ourselves to seeing what is going on in us, as it is going on. We might think that simply to be would not involve us in any character-training, but in Buddhism we discover that only the developed character has the capacity simply to be. Everybody else is too readily panicked by circumstances to be able to remain calm in the midst of the whirlwind of life. The effort that it takes simply to sit still is a good measure of the extent to which we have become alienated from our true nature.

So the practice of Right Effort, of tending the spiritual fire, of learning to sit still no matter what wind may blow up, is the basic training of the spiritual aspirant. It gives us the ability to operate effectively under fire, as it were. When Mahatma Gandhi founded his first Ashram at Ahmedabad in 1915 he made it plain that the Ashram would be open to anybody who was willing to abide by its rules, irrespective of caste. A number of local people gave financial support to the project and it got off to a good start. A few months later an Untouchable family applied to join and Gandhi accepted them. Suddenly, all financial support to the project stopped. Gandhi had anticipated this possibility and told his companions that if the project were brought to a halt by this boycott, they were not to leave Ahmedabad, but were all to go and live in the Untouchables' quarter themselves. Money ran out. When the ashram treasurer came to Gandhi and said that they had nothing for the next month, Gandhi became quiet and simply said again, 'Then we shall go to the Untouchables' quarter.' A few days later an unknown donor arrived and made a gift of 13000 rupees – enough to support the main expenses of the ashram for many months and so the project was saved.

The world needs spiritual leadership. The kind of leadership I am referring to is not necessarily a matter of stirring preaching from pulpits, but is rather to be found in the kind of stillness that Gandhi evinced in this moment of crisis. In a life like his there were innumerable such moments. They all called for inner stillness. Gandhi had his fire under control. The great Buddhist teachers I have been fortunate to meet had the same quality. If we are going to change the world, the peace starts within ourselves.

Right Mindfulness

Mindfulness really means remembrance. The point which I think the Buddha is making in setting these two items, Effort and Mindfulness, next to each other in the Eightfold Path is exactly the same point as he is making with the Second and Third Noble Truths.

We meet with affliction. We react. The first moment of this reaction is beyond our control. There is therefore no shame in either perceiving affliction or in the the first impulse of response. It is at the next step that the will can come into play. Effort is required to notice what is happening. That is the sixth step of the Eightfold Path. As soon as we notice our reaction we are faced with choice. If I feel angry, say, what will I do with this feeling?

To be mindful is to keep in mind. This operates in two different ways. On the one hand, what has arisen is contained and not allowed to spill out in a destructive way. On the other hand, wholesome states are cultivated. New ones are planted in the garden of the mind and we help them to grow and flourish. The juxtaposition of the wholesome and the unwholesome is the means to hand for managing the mind. If an unwholesome state, like greed, say, arises, it is no use resorting to denial. Pretending that it is not there really just leaves it outside conscious control and is an abdication of responsibility. Besides, denial – dishonesty – is a second weed alongside the first one. What is needed is to bring up a wholesome state alongside it. We learn to love our greed, but not to indulge it. We learn to love the child within us and we do not let the child get burned. We can look after our greed, or our grief, or our hate, or whatever it is in an appropriate way.

Another important aspect of mindfulness is to live in the

present moment. A freshness of perception is possible to us that most people only rarely experience. Enhanced awareness of the immediate natural environment is a very powerful healing influence upon the wounded psyche. To gaze at the setting sun, to touch a flower, really to hear the bird sing or to feel the weight of a stone in your hand is to come in contact with reality in a way that little else can match. In such perfect moments, we are fulfilling our purpose in being here.

Mindfulness is more, however, than acute awareness and observation. It is also the practice of faith. To be mindful is to keep in mind. What is to be kept in mind is some sense of the vertical dimension, the larger story, the possibility of transcendence. It does not really matter a great deal what form of words one uses for this. In Buddhism a great many formulas exist to serve this purpose. Such formulas are sometimes called *mantras*. A mantra is a word or phrase which is held in mind to protect the mind from unwholesome influences and to cultivate awareness of the higher purpose. A mantra is a spell. Mostly people live in a kind of trance. The mantra is a spell which breaks the trance.

Mindfulness is taking refuge. This phrase is congruent with the imagery of nirodha, already discussed, which implies taking shelter. Refuge is kept in mind by means of a phrase which expresses commitment. Thus the word 'Buddha' alone may be used. Another very commonly used formula is *Namo Amida Buddha*, or some variant thereon which is the mantra of Amida Buddha. Another is *Om Mani Padme Hum* which is the mantra of Quan Yin, the Bodhisattva of Great Compassion. These phrases are invocations. They conjure up particular associations in the mind and so act as cultivation tools of great power. For Buddhists, the story of Amida Buddha is the big story *par excellence*. It symbolises what the spiritual path is all about, namely the salvation of all beings and the creation of a pure land of bliss where all are able to progress to the fulfilment of their highest potential. To recite *Namo Amida Bu'*, therefore, is to affirm one's connection to the biggest story of all. It helps us wake up to our real reason for being here. Simply to keep a particular mantra in mind for as much of the day as possible and to recite it out loud frequently may be sufficient formal practice. The effect of this practice should, however, also be visible in the way we live our lives. To say the words is important, but then they must be put into practice.[1]

Mindfulness which is simply a technique can aid inner healing, but it does not go very deep. The really deep mindfulness comes out of conviction – inner change – a kind of catharsis. Enlightenment is a cathartic experience: an inner cleansing. There is no way that we can ensure that such an experience will occur. Often it is triggered by something unexpected. Sometimes it comes out of a feeling of contrition. Sometimes out of gratitude or grief. The emotional element is never missing. The fire of enlightenment is kindled from the fire of our passion. It is only strong authentic emotion that has the power to penetrate to the core of our being. No intellectual procedure will ever reach deep enough.

One day recently I was tripped by a chance event into contact with a deep grief buried in my memory. I was far from understanding the whole of what I experienced in the terrible few hours that followed. I wept copiously and rendingly. In the room where I was there is a cabinet within which is housed our household shrine. It is about one metre high. There are two doors on the front which close. When the doors are open the shrine is open to the room. When the doors are shut, it is an attractive Chinese cabinet with a design of twigs, blossom and birds painted in gold lacquer on a red background. I am very familiar with this piece of furniture which has shared our house with us for many years and, because of its purpose, holds a special place in our lives .

On this occasion, however, I had a surprise. In the midst of my weeping I looked up at the cabinet which was closed and I saw the birds fly. It was simply that the vividness of my perception was so greatly enhanced that the whole design stood out in three dimensions to my eye. The birds were in space and for all that my brain told me that this was a flat design painted on wood, I experienced it as alive as if they were real birds in a real tree. More so, in fact. I was quite startled. This startled feeling revealed to me not that something was wrong, but how much had been missing before.

After deep cathartic experience we may be surprised to look around the familiar sights in our environment and see them as if for the first time. On the occasion I have just mentioned, the effect was brief. In a major enlightenment experience, however, this condition of brilliant reality can persist for weeks or even months. Perhaps there are some accomplished practitioners for whom it is their all-the-time experience. Perhaps the Buddha was one such.

On other occasions when I have experienced other awakenings, similar phenomena have been apparent. The environment around one turns to fire and ice. Everything is transformed by an unexpected radiance and the feeling of rightness is complete. Even though the initial effect fades after a few weeks or months, one never returns to how one was before. Something is different inside. This 'something different' becomes a constant companion. We all have this vividness available to us all the time, but mostly, unfortunately, people live in what the Christian writer C. S. Lewis called the 'shadowlands'.

Mindfulness, then, does not just mean awareness. It is not just a matter of becoming scientifically objective. Mindfulness means to recollect our true purpose and deeply and fully live all that that entails. Remembering that there is a higher, nobler life available than that of subjection to base desires and ego maintenance, frees us to be happy. We rise above the inevitable afflictions that flow into our lives. If we have something more important to base ourselves upon, then the hurts and assaults of circumstance do not have such effect. It is not so difficult to know what we should be doing and to do it. For a long time we have been seeking an impossible immunity to the ups and downs of life, and have found ourselves repeatedly capsized as a result. Our efforts have been misdirected. There is, however, another better way that does work.

Much modern psychology asserts that values are completely relative and that we should (sic) get away from a life based on 'shoulds' and 'oughts'. The germ of truth in this idea is that many people are seriously oppressed by their fear of what others will think about them. To live our lives just trying to appease other people is surely a recipe for disaster. On the other hand, realising this should not send us to the opposite equally pernicious extreme of thinking that it does not matter what we do. It is very obvious that some courses of action do have destructive consequences. Some stories are bad stories and it is important that we do not get recruited by them.

The Third Noble Truth tells us that the fire of craving is mastered by bringing to mind what is lovely and satisfying. Yesterday I was walking into town on my way to meet a friend. I was walking quite slowly. There was no hurry. I had left in plenty of time so that I could fully experience walking. It was getting dark and there was a slight chill in the air. It was very pleasant to notice the other people all going about their business. Overhead, the sky was turning a deep ultramarine blue as the light faded away. My footfall on the pavement was gentle. I enjoyed my walk.

To act mindfully means to remember to enjoy the simple things that we do. To enjoy walking enriches our lives greatly since, unless we have serious health problems, we all spend some time walking. Take my hand and we will walk together. We will look at flowers and smile at passers-by. Our walking will be like a beautiful song, a melody that flows on without haste. The point is not to get somewhere. The point is to enjoy something lovely and satisfying. If we do so, then we are fulfilling the higher purpose.

Mindfulness, therefore, is to be happy. It is not so much the case that by overcoming craving we will overcome dukkha and find release from suffering. It is more the case that the energy provoked by dukkha will be continuously converted into bliss. We do not like to admit that we have been wrong or that we have made ourselves suffer unnecessarily. When we are first around happy people who practise mindfulness, we may start to hate them! 'Why are they smiling all the time?' we say to ourselves viciously. We find ourselves picking fault with all sorts of trivial things in an attempt to discredit what they are doing. All this, however, is really quite unnecessary. We have the option to be happy if we choose. The cost may be that we have to give up everything that we have used to defend ourselves with in the past, but this is a small price.

Kondañña was made so happy by the Buddha's teaching because it was attainable. He felt happy straight away and he felt confident that he would be able to continue to practise in this way. He would not forget.

· 28 ·

Right Samadhi

Now we come to the quintessence of the Buddha's teaching. It is very easy sometimes to begin to think that what the Buddha was describing was a kind of dry psychological technique. In fact what he offered was a transformative vision opening on to an authentic life. It is the fate of most innovators in the realm of psychology and spirituality that those who count themselves the truest disciples enshrine the founders' innovations without ever realising the source of the innovativeness. When the Buddha said that he had no teachers, he was not being literally accurate in a historical sense. He had had at least two important teachers. He had gone beyond them however, to the point where he saw for himself. He was authentic. He hoped his own disciples would become authentic in the same way, but he could not do it for them.

The Buddha's cousin, Ananda, accompanied him everywhere he went and was present at every talk he gave. Ananda knew all the Buddha's teachings off by heart. However, Ananda was not enlightened during the Buddha's lifetime. From this we know that the enlightenment of Buddhism is not a matter of learning or believing a doctrine. It is an experience. The very extent of Ananda's knowledge may well have obstructed his final enlightenment. Twenty years after the Buddha died, Ananda was enlightened after a dialogue with the Buddha's successor, Kashyapa. It is said that Ananda was eventually able to enter the room of the teachings by appearing in a very small body and entering through the keyhole.

We can imagine that Ananda must have attracted a great deal of envy, being always at the Buddha's side. Ananda was handsome and his brilliant intellect was greatly admired. As soon as the Buddha was dead, however, the other monks called Ananda before them and found a long list of things to criticise him for publicly. Pride in intellect stands in the way of enlightenment. It also attracts envy. Ananda had to chop down the mast to which he had metaphorically nailed his colours, to eat humble pie and genuinely assume a smaller form before he could enter the storehouse of the Dharma. In the story of Ananda, as recorded by Dhyana Master Keizan, it says: Ananda was fond of intellectual learning, and that is why he had not yet truly realised enlightenment. Shakyamuni, on the other hand, cultivated energy, whereby he attained true enlightenment.

Many of the people whom the Buddha called to be his disciples were already people with a considerable achievement and following of their own. He called people who had their own light. The aim of Buddhism is not to produce replica Buddhas, but to enable each person to find their light. On the other hand, for people who have achieved something there is always a danger of pride in achievement. Like Ananda, they may have to find a small body to replace their inflated one. Kondañña was able to understand directly because he had no difficulty in admitting he had been wrong.

By the night of his enlightenment the Buddha-to-be was almost completely alone. He had left everyone. Only the milk maid Sujata was still supporting him. Indeed, it was she who had brought him back from the brink of total isolation. It was she, in fact, who showed him the thing he really needed to see. We read of the Buddha's four sights – the invalid, the old person, the corpse and the wandering holy man – that inspired his going forth from the palace. The sight of Sujata's unaffected kindness was the fifth and most important sight, the one which precipitated enlightenment. Everybody else only showed the Buddha actions which were tainted with greed, hate or delusion. There was always an ulterior motive. The most elevated spiritual practices were still just ways of getting something and so were tainted with greed to get salvation, hatred for the flesh and the delusion of ego. Sujata was on the way to give her offering to the forest gods when she saw Gautama in need. Without a second thought she gave him the food. It was an authentic action. That was what he had been looking for all these years.

Action free of greed, hate and delusion became the weapon with which Gautama knew he could combat all the afflictions of the world.

This was then deeply confirmed for him on the night of his enlightenment by a vision. He had the vision of Mara's host being transformed into celestial flowers. Samadhi means concentration or rapture and refers to the vision of the purpose of life. Mara represents everything that tends toward death. Mara's representatives are all the instances of inauthentic action that crowd our ordinary lives. Newly armed with the confidence of realness, Gautama saw them all transformed into opportunities for spiritual growth. This vision was the samadhi of the Buddha. The basic meaning of the term samadhi is concentration, but to say that the samadhis of Buddhism are concentrations is a bit like saying that the works of Shakespeare are books: true, but not revealing the quality that matters. The Buddha's enlightenment is a visionary experience.

There are many indications in the texts that visionary experience was not simply something that happened to the Buddha once and for all. The transformative vision is part and parcel of the Buddha's practice on-goingly. The modern person may also be inclined to read the passages about the Buddha's converse with gods and *devas* in this way. Enlightenment changes what a person sees and experiences. The fact that modern people prefer to call visions 'inner' experiences is simply a contemporary convention of speech. A vision is certainly not experienced inwardly. When a person sees a god, the god stands before them and is in no sense 'inner'. The Buddha often talked with gods, visited heavens and preached to assemblies which included celestials as well as humans. These details are not just a superstitious addition by the Buddha's biographers. They are an indication of the quality of his lived experience. To be enlightened is to talk daily with the gods and to visit the heavens at will. In the Mahayana approach to Buddhism, many of the texts are simply attempts to give some indication of the nature of these visionary experiences. There is something which is passed down outside the scriptures that will never be available simply through reading books. But the books, nonetheless, are replete with indications of its nature for those willing to risk themselves.

The eighth step of the Eightfold Path, therefore, is authentic vision. What distinguishes an authentic vision from any other sort of vision? An authentic vision is inspired, not constructed. There is no point in trying to have the same vision that Siddhartha had, for instance.

There is a sutra called *The Sutra on Visualisation of the Buddha of Infinite Life.*[1] This includes the story of Queen Vaidehi. Vaidehi was the consort of King Bimbisara, a patron of the Buddha, who had been overthrown by his son Ajatashatru. Queen Vaidehi had interceded between her husband and son and had tried to thwart Ajatashatru's intention to starve his father to death. In consequence she herself was imprisoned without food to await the same fate. In the extremity of her distress she addressed a prayer to the Buddha who she knew would be preaching at a place not far away. The Buddha and two of his disciples appeared to her: 'he was the colour of purple gold and was seated on a lotus flower of a hundred jewels. He was attended by Maudgalyayana on his left and Ananda on his right. Shakra, Bramah, the guardian gods of the world and other devas were in the air about him. Scattering heavenly blossoms like rain, they paid homage to the Buddha.'[2] Such was the first vision she saw.

Then she again falls into tears. She laments her fate and particularly the fact of having a son who is so wicked as to be in process of murdering both his parents. She feels a point of kinship here with the Buddha since he, the Buddha, has a cousin, Devadatta, who has tried, unsuccessfully, to overthrow his leadership of the Buddhist community and assassinate him. She longs for a better world in which one will not have to 'hear evil words or see wicked people'. She agonises over the question that so many human beings have asked in so many circumstances: What have I done to deserve this? She does not, however, do so in the spirit of asserting her innocence or of rhetorically expressing her indignation. She kneels down to repent.

At this point there is a flood of light in which she sees buddha lands in every direction. She has an authentic vision. The vision emerges from the depth of her emotion (samudaya) which, in turn emerges from the extremity of her plight (dukkha). From amongst these varied buddha lands, she chooses the Land of Amitayus, the Buddha of Infinite Life, the Western Land of Utmost Bliss. This is the story of how Vaidehi found peace and meaning in the time prior to her death.

It is easy to see the moral of the story. There is not much worse that can happen to a person than to be stripped of everything important and slowly destroyed by their only child, while knowing that the same thing is happening to the spouse they love. This must rank at the extremity of torments. Yet in such a place, Vaidehi, could find peace through samadhi which became possible through her faith in the Buddha and her willingness to let go of any sense of self-righteousness. Abandon self and have faith. The vision was triggered by an act of contrition. If a woman of no particular spiritual advancement could, simply through faith, reach such a point in such an extremity, then, in principle, there is nothing that the human spirit cannot surmount.

The Sutra then goes on, interestingly, to describe a means to have a vision approximating to that which Vaidehi experienced. This description is a kind of do-it-by-numbers version which begins with 'Visualise a sunset . . .' Such an approach provides us with a means to achieve a replica via the imagination of Vaidehi's experience. Of course, there is as much in common between this replica and Vaidehi's original as there is between a real tree and a plastic model of one. The purpose of giving a description of how to achieve such an imitation is simply to inspire people to go and find their own vision.

We can read about the vision received by Gautama on the night of his enlightenment, or by Queen Vaidehi prior to her death or, indeed, the visions of Mary the mother of Jesus or of the saints of any religion. Such visions are part of the conversion experience of all spiritual traditions. What matters is not so much the content of the precise vision – whether we see angels or bodhisattvas, for instance – as whether the vision is authentic. Does it come from the true spontaneous source? Does it show a true path? Is it both inwardly and outwardly authentic? If so, then it is a genuine spiritual experience. The real measure of such an event, however, is not in the experience itself but in the effect it has upon the life of the person.

A spiritual teacher will have no end of people come along and describe all manner of visionary experiences. Sometimes the motive of the teller is simply to impress, in which case the telling, let alone the vision itself, is inauthentic. Sometimes the person genuinely wants to know what the meaning may be of what they have experienced. The test of validity, however, always lies in the lived life. If a vision leads a person to a more unified, wholesome, constructive and kind way of living, then the vision is sound. If it leads to estrangement, artificiality, pride or confusion, then it is delusion. Not all visions are the same. The Buddha specifies *right* samadhi in the Eightfold Path because there are also wrong samadhis that do no good.

Samadhi, right or wrong, has great spiritual power. Wrong samadhi may lead to the most terrible consequences. This kind of negative enlightenment is what leads to a person becoming a megalomaniac. Hitler and Stalin certainly had their visions and great powers of concentration. The results, however, were terrible. The highest and the lowest lives are inspired by visions.

· 29 ·

The Necessity of Suffering

We are now in a position to look back upon the Four Noble Truths and to draw out some implications. We have seen that this is a four-step teaching. The first step is the inevitability of affliction. The second is the naturalness of the arising of passion in us when affliction is perceived. The third step is to do with the art of mastering that passion and rendering it useful. The fourth step is the path or purposeful life which unfolds for a person who has mastered their passions in the manner prescribed.

We have seen that this interpretation leads to the rejection of many commonly made assertions about what the Buddha is supposed to have taught. In particular we have rejected all of the following propositions:

1 That the Buddha taught the cessation of suffering.
2 That dukkha refers primarily to mental suffering.
3 That the doctrine of rebirth is an essential implication of the Four Noble Truths.
4 That passion and enlightenment are mutually exclusive.
5 That buddhas are not sentient and do not have personal problems after their enlightenment.
6 That the Eightfold Path leads to enlightenment.
7 That attaining enlightenment necessarily takes a long time.
8 That the Second Noble Truth is about the cause of suffering.
9 That the Third Noble Truth is about bringing the cause of suffering to an end.
10 That nirvana means extinction.

We have seen that enlightenment is a cathartic experience which occurs when a person deeply realises the extent to which they have been running away from reality and surrenders to this possibility of living a full and meaningful life in whatever circumstances they find themselves. Such an awakening reveals to them the compelling desirability of the 'noble life' and the corresponding necessity for the form of self-training implied by the Third Noble Truth. Such an experience stops a person in their tracks. They discover a deep inner stillness, the mind becoming like crystal clear water and, as the inner interference drops away, they experience the world around them transfigured in radiance. This experience is called perceiving a 'buddha land'. It occurs naturally to many people on their deathbed. It is available, however, at any time. The sincere spiritual seeker is likely to have at least one and sometimes several profound experiences of this kind which will stand out as landmarks in their lifetime. Although such major awakenings fade, they leave the person significantly changed. Their personality has been magnetised. Their energies are more unified and their senses more acute. Life becomes more vibrant in every way.

Such a transformation inspires inner stillness and outer purpose. Nirvana is the mastery of passion by sheltering it from ego-driven disturbance. Enlightenment is cathartic, both because it involves a climb down by the ego and because it involves an opening up to the impact of affliction not just upon oneself, but upon everyone. It most characteristically manifests as a profoud sense of relief: a 'who would have thought that everything is so wonderful just as it is!' One abandons one's individual concerns as one becomes carried up into the bigger story. In this bigger story both bliss and suffering have their proper parts: a time to be born and a time to die.

The practices of Buddhism which have come down through the centuries are very compatible with the interpretation of the Dharma that we have arrived at. In fact they are, in a number of respects, more compatible with this interpretation than with that of the traditional commentaries. It may well be that the Buddha's message has been better preserved in the practices than in the texts. Bodhidharma's assertion that the truth is handed down outside the scriptures may be more literally true than many have realised.

The Buddha, we know, rejected the extremes of self-indulgence and of asceticism. However, there is no doubt that he also encouraged a number of practices that are in the nature of privations. Fasting every day after noon is not designed for comfort. Begging for your food and going hungry if none is forthcoming would be a strange practice, if the aim were to eliminate suffering from your life. The Buddha did intend that his followers experience a certain amount of adversity daily. some suffering was part and parcel of his prescription. He did not encourage extremes, but he did encourage a degree of experimentation with fasting and with reducing the amount of sleep taken, and generally advocated an attitude of stoicism in regard to unanticipated misfortunes that might arise. Even the fundamental practice of meditation involves sitting in a posture that most people find uncomfortable until they have been doing it for many years and staunchly resisting every impulse to move. This practice is a training in fortitude as well as a quest for insight.

If we consider once again our summary of the Four Noble Truths at the beginning of this chapter, we can see why this might be so. If the Four Noble Truths are to be read in this A leads to B leads to C leads to D fashion, then it is clear that the desirable goal, namely the path, depends upon the initial factor, namely affliction. No suffering, no passion. No passion, no mastery thereof. No mastery, no path. From this perspective we can see affliction, dukkha, not as an unavoidable evil, let alone as the curse of mankind that the path is designed to eliminate, but rather as the essential starting point without which the spiritual life would not be possible. Suffering is necessary.

Let us put this another way. The analogy used throughout this study is that of fire. This analogy was given by the Buddha himself. The spiritual life consists of mastery of the fire. Affliction is the fuel for the fire. If I need a fire I need fuel. The disciple of the Buddha tends his or her inner fire. This fire needs a supply of fuel. The fuel is the affliction in the world. In order to get the fire to the appropriate heat there needs to be the right amount of fuel. Sometimes this is readily to hand. The circumstances of life provide plenty to work on. The koan arises naturally in daily life, as they say in Soto Zen temples. Sometimes, however, the practitioner needs to feed the fire. This is where a modest degree of privation or ascetic practice starts to make sense. Not too much and not too little.

This way of thinking is completely congruent with the behaviour of serious Buddhist practitioners as we witness it in the world today and as it has no doubt always been. The practitioner tends the inner fire. This is not the way *toward* enlightenment. It already is enlightened action. Keeping the fire healthy and under control is a matter of balance – a middle way. In this process, affliction plays an essential part.

This way of thinking suggests a significant shift of perspective. Buddhism is not about eliminating suffering. It is about noble living. Noble living requires the existence of a moderate amount of hardship. This has nothing to do with punishment and even less to do with indulgence. It is simply a practical matter. Suffering is no longer a problem, it is absorbed into the noble life by being given its proper role which is to feed the spirit. This is only possible for a person who has learned the art of husbanding passion. The Third Noble Truth is thus the vital one in terms of practice. The Third leads to the Fourth, not *vice versa*. If the traditional interpretation were correct they would probably have been said the other way round.

This rehabilitation of suffering in the scheme of things does not mean that Buddhists seek martyrdom. That would be an extreme. Martyrdom is a rare phenomenon in Buddhism. There have been Buddhist martyrs, but they are not particularly glorified. Suffering is not glorified. It has its place, that is all. Suffering is not a measure of our virtue and is not to be carried to extreme. That would, the Buddha says, be quite counterproductive.

When the bodhisattva vows to take all beings with him to the other shore, what is implied? If the other shore is not the abolition of suffering in the world, what is it? What sort of world are these Buddhists trying to create? The Buddhist ideal is summed up in the two key adjectives 'noble' and 'true'. A buddha is not someone who has no personal problems and certainly not someone who never suffers. To stand on the other shore is not so much to go to a different world as to see this world from a different standpoint. The bodhisattva is not saying, 'This world is terrible: let me help you escape from it.' He or she is saying, 'Come and look at it this way and you will have a quite different and much more satisfactory experience.'

When Shakyamuni was enlightened he is supposed to have said, 'When I am enlightened, all beings are enlightened with me.' What can this mean? When a person is enlightened, they see the noble truth of others' lives as well as of their own. The person who practises Right View, listens deeply and, like Quan Yin, hears the cry in the person's heart. When we perceive a person in this way, we cannot help respecting them and seeing how that cry expresses a deep and universal truth. We see how their life naturally grows out of their struggle. We see that they are also noble in their own way and that their truth is unfolding as it should.

It was because the Buddha had this deep empathy for everyone who came to see him that he was able to be such an effective teacher – or perhaps nowadays we might say, therapist. He could tune into the other person's world. When we look at a person superficially, we may find much to criticise. We cannot see why they act in such a foolish way. If only they would see sense and realise what we can see so clearly. When we look deeply, however, we get a quite different feeling for the person. The reason for their foibles becomes clear to us. We can imagine ourselves being just the same, had we been born with their temperament and brought up in their circumstances. The deeper our empathy, the more readily comes our positive regard.

While we think that enlightenment is total freedom from suffering, we cannot understand the meaning of the Buddha's statement, since the world is undeniably full of suffering beings. If we abandon this idea, however, and see that affliction has a necessary part to play in the sustenance of the noble life, this obstacle dissolves. Buddha was not saying, 'When I am free from suffering all beings are free from suffering.' He was saying, 'When I am noble and true, all beings are noble and true.' A noble person is one who sees the nobility of others – the courage of ordinary lives. To see what is noble and true in others is not a product of seeing our own perfection so much as of seeing our own humanity. That the Buddha was enlightened does not mean that he ceased to be human – quite the contrary.

The noble life which the Buddha advocated is not dependent upon circumstances. It is easier if we have noble friends to inspire us, of course, and we are advised to seek them out, support them and associate with them, but even if we finish up, like Yelui Chu Tsai, surrounded by butchers, it is not impossible. Soon after his enlightenment, the Buddha realised that he had a job to do. He changed completely. Instead of becoming more and more isolated, as he had done before, he became more and more engaged. He reached out to everybody. He brought forth love. He touched and inspired many people. He still had a few personal matters to sort out – like his relationship with the wife and child he had deserted, the father he had defied and the mother for whom he mourned – so he got on with that, too. He started a movement which in due course needed a lot of practical organisation. A big story began to unfold that is still running. It had its ups and downs. There was a time when the Buddha so despaired of the wrangling going on among his followers that he left them to it and retired to the forest for a few months. But his capacity to keep his nerve even in this situation paid off, just as it later did when attempts were made to split the order and even to assassinate him. He had his fire and he had it under control.

If we want to see a buddha land, it is right here. This is the mandala – the big story. Nobody is excluded save by their clinging to their own little story. The gates of enlightenment are wide open. It is not a matter of accumulating merit. We are all quite acceptable to the buddhas already, just as we are. It is not a matter of eliminating grief. Grief is essential to the process of spiritual growth. It is not a matter of solving all our personal problems. They are grist to the mill. There is therefore nothing to be done other than to wake up and embrace reality and opportunity. If we do wake up, however, it is apparent that there is something to be done after all. This something is what the Four Noble Truths describe: the necessity of affliction; the value of passion; the sheltering of it from the ego wind; and the unfolding of the noble life: Right View, Right Thought, Right

Speech, Right Action, Right Livelihood, Right Effort, Right Mindfulness, and Right Samadhi. If we follow this path, the birds will sing for us more clearly than before, the sunset will be more magnificent and the peace in our heart will be fathomless.

Conclusion

The Four Noble Truths provide the basis of Buddhism. They constitute a practical approach to the problem of life. They define spirituality as the art of converting base passion into noble engagement. On the one hand, we live in a wonderful world in which there is the potential for immense satisfaction. On the other hand, at every turn we come up against obstacles, restrictions, limits and frustrations. Both these things, called 'sweet spaces' and 'bitter spaces', *sukha* and *dukkha*, are inherent aspects of existence. We live in a world which is both bliss and affliction.

Limitation is part of life and is actually the part that gives it meaning, tenor, vitality and aliveness. The affliction we come up against is the basis of our consciousness and our capacity for awareness, without which bliss would not be possible. This is the basis of the problem which constitutes our main spiritual work. We do not get everything we want. Affliction is part and parcel of life. In response to affliction, feelings arise. These feelings are capable of making our life hell. They are also an energy source which can be harnessed to put us onto a constructive life path.

The Buddha describes what such a path would be like. It would be one in which we were free from self-defeating views. Our heads would not be full of either arrogance or self-deprecation. Our thoughts, speech, and action would all flow together in a constructive way to create a positive lifestyle. This in itself brings a major degree of peace of mind. This mental cultivation however, can be carried further through right effort and mindfulness, until we enter into the condition of mind that Buddhists call samadhi: a mind which naturally finds the bliss in all the eventualities of everyday life and so enables us to fulfil our purpose in being alive.

This purpose is to contribute our energy to the creation of 'the pure land of bliss' which is not an other-worldly paradise entered after physical death, but a here and now state of psychological maturity, through which the obstacles we meet are, like the army of Mara in the Buddha's enlightenment vision, continuously transformed into celestial flowers.

This is the transformative vision offered us by the Buddha. It contains no element of escapism, nor is it dependent upon belief in a particular system of metaphysics. The poetry necessary to convey the workings of the spirit should not be reified into dogma. It is available to people of all races, classes, genders, and creeds. It is capable of translation into the language of different social groups because it speaks to the basic existential condition of our lives which transcends all membership categories.

It provides a workable basis for a therapy of individuals, families, societies and the strife torn world in which we live. Affliction is both individual and collective and so is our response to it. Buddhism is not just a private affair. It is the so very simple yet all embracing basis for the creation of mature lives and civilised societies in which harmony and awareness prevail.

I have tried to convey some of this vision. I have tried to show how it emerged from the life experience of Siddhartha Gautama who lost his mother at birth, who was driven by inner anguish to wander the world, who drove himself to the limits of endurance, who was moved to enlightenment by an act of kindness, who dedicated the remainder of his life to the service of others, and who came to be called the Buddha, but who called himself 'the one who had been there'.[1] He went to see for himself. His self-chosen epithet carries the implication of having found out the hard way.

I hope that by writing this book I have done something to counter the tendencies, on the one hand, to rarify Buddhism into an other-worldly religious system remote from the experience of you and me, and, on the other, to make of it an esoteric academic subject only accessible to holders of doctoral degrees.

The tendency to distance ourselves from the realities and hard work of life is understandable, but it cuts us off from our bliss.

The basis of this book has been the talk that Buddha gave at the very beginning of his ministry. Here we have the essence of his whole message. If we are moved by its spirit, simplicity and power, then we may follow his final advice to 'seek out our own salvation with all diligence' and to 'go forth for the benefit of the many'. The world needs people who have become fully alive. The cost of becoming so is high in that it involves facing the inherent insecurity of our situation and realising that we do not stand alone, but are indissolubly involved in the fate of one another and of the world around us. The potential reward is, however, commensurate with the cost.

The Buddha was a human being and a person with a passion. The momentum of that passion is still very much alive today.

The Text of the Buddha's Talk

SETTING IN MOTION THE WHEEL OF THE DHARMA

1 Thus have I heard. Once the 'One who Enjoys the Spoils of Victory' was staying at Isipatana near Benares.

2 He spoke to the group of five ascetics as follows: Monks, there are two extremes which one who has left the household life should not resort to.

3 What are they? One is devotion to sense desire and sense pleasure. It is demeaning. It is the way of ordinary folk. It is unworthy and unprofitable. The other is devotion to self mortification. It is painful and ignoble. It is not conducive to the real purpose of life. Giving up these extremes, the 'One who has Been There' has woken up to the middle way which provides insight and understanding and causes peace, wisdom, enlightenment and nirvana.

4 The Middle Way is the noble eight limb way of right view, right thought, right speech, right action, right livelihood, right effort, right mindfulness and right samadhi.

5 The noble truth of dukkha, affliction, is this: birth, old age, sickness, death, grief, lamentation, pain, depression, and agitation are dukkha. Dukkha is being associated with what you do not like, being separated from what you do like, and not being able to get what you want. In short, the five aggregates of grasping are dukkha.

6 The noble truth of samudaya, response to affliction, is this: it is thirst for self re-creation which is associated with greed. It lights upon whatever pleasures are to be found here and there. It is thirst for sense pleasure, for being and non-being.

7 The noble truth of nirodha, containment, is this: it is the

complete capturing of that thirst. It is to let go of, be liberated from and refuse to dwell in the object of that thirst.

8 The noble truth of marga, the right track, is this: it is the noble eight-limb way, namely right view, right thought, right speech, right action, right livelihood, right effort, right mindfulness and right samadhi.

9 'This is the noble truth of affliction' – this was the insight, understanding, wisdom, knowledge and clarity which arose in me about things I had not been taught.

'Affliction should be understood to be a noble truth' – this was the insight, understanding, wisdom, knowledge and clarity which arose in me about things I had not been taught.

'Full understanding of affliction as a noble truth has dawned' – this was the insight, understanding, wisdom, knowledge and clarity which arose in me about things I had not been taught.

10 'This is the noble truth of response' – this was the insight, understanding, wisdom, knowledge and clarity which arose in me about things I had not been taught.

'Response should be understood to be a noble truth' – this was the insight, understanding, wisdom, knowledge and clarity which arose in me about things I had not been taught.

'Full understanding of response as a noble truth has dawned' – this was the insight, understanding, wisdom, knowledge and clarity which arose in me about things I had not been taught.

11 'This is the noble truth of containment' – this was the insight, understanding, wisdom, knowledge and clarity which arose in me about things untaught.

'Containment should be understood to be a noble truth' – this was the insight, understanding, wisdom, knowledge and clarity which arose in me about things untaught.

'Full understanding of containment as a noble truth has dawned' – this was the insight, understanding, wisdom, knowledge and clarity which arose in me about things untaught.

12 'This is the noble truth of the path' – this was the insight, understanding, wisdom, knowledge and clarity which arose in me about things untaught.

'This path should be understood to be a noble truth' – this was the insight, understanding, wisdom, knowledge and clarity which arose in me about things untaught.

'Full understanding of the path as a noble truth has dawned' – this was the insight, understanding, wisdom, knowledge and clarity which arose in me about things untaught.

13 As long as I had not got a completely clear insight and understanding in all these three ways about each of these Four Noble Truths, I could not be sure that there was anyone in the world, divine or human, who had woken up to the highest and most complete enlightenment.

14 However, when my insight and understanding had become completely clear in all these twelve turnings of the wheel, then I knew for sure that there was someone in the world who had woken up to the highest and most complete enlightenment. Then I knew that the liberation of my mind was unassailable. This is the last step. There is no further step.

15 When the Victorious One had said this, the five monks were filled with joy. In one of them, Kondañña, the pure Dharma Eye was completely opened. He saw that whatever can arise can be contained.

16 When the Victorious One had turned the wheel of the Dharma in this way the spirits of the earth cried out: Near Benares, in the Deer Park at Isipatana, the wheel of the highest Dharma has been turned and it cannot now be turned back by anyone, human or divine, anywhere in the world.

17, 18, 19 This cry resounded throughout the heavenly realms. The earth shook. An immeasurable light was now released into the world.

20 Then the Blessed One said: Venerable Kondañña has understood. And from that day on he was given the name 'He who understood'.

[*Samyutta Nikaya* 61.11]

Glossary

Terms of eastern origin are Sanskrit unless otherwise stated

Abhidharma: early books of psychological analysis of the Buddha's teachings.

Amitabha: Buddha of Infinite Light. Also called Amida.

Amitayus: Buddha of Limitless Life. In China *Amitabha* and *Amitayus* become a single figure called Amida.

anatma: no-self. This is the teaching of the Buddha upon the impossibility of creating a self which is beyond the reach of *dukkha* (q.v.)

anicca: transience, impermanence.

arhat: an enlightened person who may or may not be a teacher of others. *cf. buddha, bodhisattva.*

aryan: noble.

Avalokiteshvara: the Bodhisattva of Compassion. In Chinese called Quan Yin.

avidya: spiritual blindness. Ignorance. From *a-* (not) and *vidya* (see).

bodhi: spiritual awakening.

bodhichitta: the thought of enlightenment. Consciousness of the higher purpose of life.

bodhisattva: (1) one on the way toward enlightenment; (2) an enlightened person devoted to the spiritual welfare of others.

buddha: an awakened one. Somebody who has achieved enlightenment through their own experience and imparts enlightenment to others.

deva: a radiant being; a god.

Dharma: the Buddhist teaching.

dhyana: meditative absorption.

dukkha: affliction, bitter space.

karma: action and the traces

thereof left in our mentality.
All wilful acts leave their
mark on the actor. Once
we have done something
we are liable to do it
again.

koan (Japanese): the nub of a
spiritual issue or obstacle
that a practitioner tries to
penetrate. A spiritual
exercise based upon
contemplating the
enlightenment experience of
a former master.

kshanti: patience, endurance,
capacity. The ability to take
things in one's stride. One
of the qualities of a
bodhisattva.

lama: (Tibetan) spiritual
teacher.

mahasattva: great being. See
also *bodhisattva*.

Mahayana: the schools of
Buddhism which assert that
all beings are on the way to
becoming buddhas or,
latently, already are
buddhas.

mandala: a symetrical
diagramme symbolising
spiritual harmony.

mantra: a word or phrase
which is held in mind to
protect the mind from
unwholesome influences
and to cultivate awareness
of the higher purpose of
life.

Mara: death, a figure
appearing in Buddhist texts
who personifies death.

marga: path, way.

nirodha: to contain, confine,
or capture.

nirvana: the condition of
spiritual maturity in which
one's passions are
mastered.

rupa: form, appearance.

saddhu: holy man, priest,
mendicant monk.

samadhi: concentration, the
unified mind of the
awakened person.

samjna: entrancement, the
mental operation that links
an 'incoming' stimulus with
material already stored in
the mind.

samskara: mental
programming, internal
formation.

samudaya: that which arises
along with something else.
Feelings.

sangha: strictly this means the
community of monks and
nuns; more generally it
refers to the Buddhist
community, past and
present.

skandhas: the five steps in the
process whereby we grasp
at and identify with the
impulses that arise in
response to the outside
world. The skandhas are

listed as *rupa, vedana, samjna, samskara* and *vijnana* (q.v.).

shamatha: stopping; meditation which brings tranquility to the mind.

Soto (Japanese): a branch of the Zen school.

sukha: happiness; *su-* (sweet) + *-kha* (space, gap, interlude). Compare *dukkha* (q.v.).

Sukhavati: the Land of Bliss which, according to a story told by the Buddha, is where Amida presides over a land of plenty in which spiritual progress is easier to accomplish. Also called the Pure Land.

sutra: literally a thread; by extension, the thread of a story. The texts recording the actions and sayings of the Buddha and his followers are called *Sutras* (*sutta* in Pali).

Tathagata: the epithet the Buddha gave himself. The precise implication is difficult to determine with certainty, but, perhaps: 'having gone to that', i.e. having been to see for himself.

Theravada: 'the way of the elders'. A school of Buddhism found in southern Asian countries and now in the west.

vedana: reaction. Construing something a certain way, we react.

vijnana: ordinary consciousness in which people experience themselves as 'subjects' separate from the 'objects' they perceive, hence 'observer-consciousness'.

Vinaya: books of monastic discipline.

Zen (Japanese): a school of Buddhism which emphasises meditation practice found primarily in China, Japan, Korea, Vietnam and western countries. The word derives from *dhyana* (q.v.).

Notes

Chapter One: *No Pearl without Grit*

1. The term Buddha, spelt with a capital B, designates the teacher Gautama Siddhartha, founder of the Buddhist religion, who lived in India some twenty-five centuries ago. The term buddha without a capital signifies any similarly enlightened teacher. The word 'buddha' means 'awakened'.

Chapter Three: *Misunderstanding Buddhism*

1. *Dhammacakkappavattana-sutta*, *Samyutta Nikaya* 56,11. The Sutra on the Setting in Motion of the Wheel of the Dharma. The image of a wheel with four main spokes representing the Four Noble Truths and eight spokes altogether, representing the Eightfold Path, has become the best known symbol of Buddhism. The wheel turns, but at its centre there is a still point. This represents the union of buddha-nature (inner stillness) and skilful means (outer activity).

Chapter Five: *Introducing the Four Noble Truths*

1. Manné in her doctoral thesis, *Debates and Case Histories in the Pali Canon* (University of Utrecht, 1992), compiles evidence that the common schema of four grades, namely: stream-enterer, once-returner, non-returner and *arhat*, is a later development to accommodate ideas about reincarnation. Initially the Buddhists distinguished simply *arhats*, who like Kondañña understood completely, from the rest of the faithful who had entered the stream but did not yet fully understand.

Chapter Ten: *Freedom to Feel*

1. Dogen (1200–53) transmitted the Soto School of Zen from China to Japan. This and many other similarly down to earth comments are to be found in the collection of his talks known as *Shobogenzo-zuimonki*. This has been translated by Shohaku Okamura in a small volume distributed in the UK by Wisdom Books.

2. It has become a point of doctrine for a number of schools of Buddhism that all living creatures are divided into two categories, viz. sentient beings and buddhas. This book argues that that categorisation is invalid and pernicious. The Buddha was human in the fullest sense of the word.

3. The term consciousness is here used in its common usage sense and not in the technical sense found in philosophical discourse.

4. An informative book is Worden's *Grief Counselling and Grief Therapy* (London: Routledge, 1987) which also has an extensive bibliography and the work of Colin Murray Parkes (*e.g. Bereavement: Studies of grief in adult life*, New York: International Universities Press, 1972) is well known. The term 'grief reaction' would not be a bad translation of the term *dukkha samudaya*. The second Noble Truth is *inter alia* about grief reaction.

5. See Marris, *Loss and Change*, London: Routledge & Kegan Paul, 1986.

6. She has been in the *Traya-strimsa* Heaven since seven days after his birth. The name means 'Threefold Women's Heaven'.

Chapter Eleven: *Asking for Help*

1. *Avidya*. This Buddhist interpretation has a good deal in common, if we adjust the terminology, with Rogers' theory of 'organismic self'. Thus: 'when a person is functioning fully, there are no barriers, no inhibitions, which prevent the full experiencing of whatever is organismically present (Rogers 1980, p. 128). Experiencing and acting are not the same, however. Rogers took for granted a level of behavioural discipline, whereas Buddhism spells this out.

2. The skills associated with regulating emotional distance between a person and the stimulus material associated with a particular emotional state are discussed in T. J. Scheff, *Catharsis, Healing, Ritual and Drama*, published by University of California Press (1979) and in the contributions by Beech and by Leijssen in

Brazier (editor) *Beyond Carl Rogers*, published by Constable (1993).

Chapter Twelve: *The Pleasure Trap*

1. The story of Bodhidharma meeting the Emperor is told in many books. An easily accessible discussion of it is to be found in chapter two of Thien-an's *Zen Philosophy, Zen Practice*, Dharma Publishing (1975). The term 'spiritual materialism' has acquired currency through Chogyam Trungpa's book *Cutting Through Spiritual Materialism*, Shambhala (1987).
2. The allegory of the burning house is taken from the Lotus Sutra, chapter 3.
3. *Samyutta Nikaya* 35, 28.
4. In Buddhist psychology the dependence of inner experience upon outer stimulation is called 'object relation'. This is explained in more detail in chapter 9 of D. Brazier, *Zen Therapy*, Constable (1995).
5. *Sandokai*. See J. Kennett, *Zen Is Eternal Life*, Dharma Publishing (1976), p. 281.
6. The most important text is the *Satipatthana Sutta. Majjhima Nikaya* 10. This has been translated by Thich Nhat Hanh as Transformation and Healing: Sutra on the four establishments of mindfulness, published by Parallax (1990).

Chapter Thirteen: *Hate and Delusion*

1. Freud wrote his paper 'The economic problem of masochism' in 1924.
2. Two translations of this work are Thomas Cleary's *No Barrier: Unlocking the Zen Koan*, published by HarperCollins (1993) and Katsuki Sekida's *Two Zen Classics* published by Weatherhill (1977).
3. See D. T. Suzuki, *Essays in Zen Buddhism (Second Series)*, (Rider, 1950), for an extensive discussion of the use of koans in Buddhist practice.

Chapter Fourteen: *Taming the Fire*

1. *Rodha* means a bank of earth, like a river bank. Later the word *rodha* was extended to mean an enclosure and so also a

prison. Payutto in *Dependent Origination: The Buddhist law of conditionality* (Buddhadhamma Foundation, 1994), takes the word as meaning 'out of prison', but this is surely incorrect since then the word would have to be *nir-rodha*. Also, a stylistic symmetry is created by the juxtaposition of *ud*, up, in the Second Noble Truth, and *ni*, down, in the Third which would disappear if nirodha were constructed from *nir*, 'without'. I can see little support either for the common interpretation of the word *nirodha* as 'cessation'.

Chapter Fifteen: *Spirit without Metaphysics*

1. W. Rahula, *What the Buddha Taught*, Gordon Fraser (1978), p. 35.
2. The Denkoroku has been translated by Thomas Cleary as *Transmission of Light*, published by North Point Press (1990) and, in contrasting style, the first 18 chapters also appear in Jiyu Kennett's *Zen Is Eternal Life* (Dharma Publishing, 1976).
3. C. N. Phuong, *Learning True Love*, Parallax (1993), p. 63.
4. K. Tanahashi & T. D. Schneider, *Essential Zen*, HarperCollins (1994), p. 123.

Chapter Sixteen: *Psychotherapy*

1. I have argued the case for seeing Buddhism as a psychotherapy elsewhere. See: 'Is Buddhism a Therapy?' *Raft: The Journal of the Buddhist Hospice Trust, 10* (1994).
2. This is known technically as 'post-traumatic stress disorder'. An interesting recent contribution to this subject which contains many views parallel to the Buddhist approach is J. Shay's *Achilles in Vietnam: Combat trauma and the undoing of character* (Simon & Schuster, 1994), which gives a valuable analysis of the effects of combat trauma on soldiers.
3. In the Setting Up of Mindfulness Sutra referred to in note 8 to chapter 11 above.

Chapter Seventeen: *Time to Stop*

1. *Selling Water by the River* was the original title of Jiyu Kennett's book *Zen Is Eternal Life*, Dharma Publishing (1976).

2. See, for instance, W. Mikulas' article 'Mindfulness, Self-control and Personal Growth', in M. G. T. Kwee (editor) *Psychotherapy, Meditation and Health* (East-West Publications, 1990), pp. 151–65.

3. The phrase Namo Amida Bu is called the *nembutsu* (in Japanese) which means Buddha-impulse or Buddha-thought. It is an expression of the fact that there is an impulse toward buddha-hood occurring in us every moment. It is also an expression of faith in the saving power of the Buddha's aspiration to help all beings.

4. See Nhat Hanh's manual of guided meditations *The Blooming of a Lotus*, Beacon Press (1993), for many similar valuable reflections.

Chapter Eighteen: *Angulimala*

1. *Majjhima Nikaya* 86

Chapter Twenty: *The Big Story*

1. See an interesting discussion of this point in chapter 7 of D. Taylor's *The Healing Power of Stories* (Gill & Macmillan, 1996).

2. The Buddha's great energy is apparent in passages such as the following: 'Then the blessed One instructed, inspired, fired and delighted the lay people of Pataligama with discussion of Dharma until far into the night.' *Mahaparinibbana Sutta, Digha Nikaya* 2.87.

Chapter Twenty-One: *Right View*

1. There is good discussion of the Buddha's view about views in Phra Khantipalo book, *Tolerance* puyblished by Rider (1964).

2. The method which the Buddha is advocating by his idea that 'all views are wrong views' is similar to the approach of those western philosophers who call their approach phenomenology. Edmund Husserl, the German philosopher who founded phenomenology, showed how, if we are to see reality, we have to 'bracket' our preconceptions. Husserl was originally a mathematician. In algebra variables are put in brackets to keep them apart from the other operations that are going on. This idea is not to be confused with 'moral relativism' which is the idea that all views

are right views, an idea that the Buddha, like any sensible person, rejected.

3. The *Zenrin* is a collection of two-line poems compiled by Toyo Eicho (1429–1504).

4. The *Bhaddekaratta Sutta, Majjhima Nikaya 131* provides a clear account of the unburdened mind. There is a translation by Bhikkhu Nanananda published by the Buddhist Publication Society (1973) under the title *Ideal Solitude*.

5. The comparison with catching a snake is found in the *Alagaddupama Sutta, Majjhima Nikaya 22*. There is a translation by Nyanaponika Thera published by the Buddhist Publication Society (1973) under the title *The Snake Simile* and another by Thich Nhat Hanh, *Thundering Silence: Sutra on Knowing the Better Way to Catch a Snake*, Parallax Press (1993).

6. A review of the background to the Zenrin can be found in Alan Watts's *The Way of Zen*, Penguin (1957). The symbol of the ox finds expression in a well known series of Zen paintings with accompanying poems known as the 'Ox Herding Pictures'. The latter can be found in translation in *Zen Flesh, Zen Bones* by Paul Reps (Penguin, 1957) and in Katsuki Sekida's *Zen Training: Methods and Philosophy*, published by Weatherhill (1985).

Chapter Twenty-Two: *Right Thought*

1. *Dhammapada* v3–5. Many translations of this favourite Buddhist anthology are available. Juan Mascaro's translation, *The Dhammapada: The Path of Freedom*, published by Penguin (1973), is easily obtained, as is Eknath Easwaran's *The Dhammapada*, published by Arkana, and there are many others.

2. Fay Weldon, 'The Enemy Within', *Prospect*, February 1997, p. 15.

3. *The Biographical Scripture of King Ashoka, Taisho 50, 2043*. A translation by Li Rongxi is published by the Numata Centre (1993).

4. R. E. Buswell *The Zen Monastic Experience* published by Princeton University Press (1992), p. 155.

5. For these observations I am indebted to Stephen Batchelor's book *Alone With Others*, Grove Press (1983).

6. The name Amida derives from the Sanskrit *Amitabha* meaning 'Buddha of infinite light' and *Amitayus*, Buddha of infinite life.

Amida, in one or other of these forms appears in a great many Buddhist scriptures. Quan Yin, the buddha or bodhisattva of great compassion is a female form in Chinese Buddhism but in India was male. His (or her) Sanskrit name is *Avalokiteshvara*. These two figures show the interaction between different spiritual traditions in their attempt to represent archetypal forces. The origins of Amida probably owe something to the Persian god of light, *Ahura Mazda*, and the female form of Quan Yin something to Marian Christian influence.

7. This is a quotation from the 25th chapter of the Lotus Sutra. This chapter of the Sutra is often treated as a scripture in its own right.

8. C. R. Rogers, 'The necessary and sufficient conditions of therapeutic personality change', *Journal of Consulting Psychology* 21, (1957), pp. 95–103.

Chapter Twenty-Three: *Right Speech*

1. This sentence is taken from the Buddhist scripture *Digha Nikaya* 1.4.

2. An account of this famous incident is given by Z. Isigami in his book *Disciples of the Buddha* published by Kosei (1989), pp. 18–19.

3. *The Sutra of Hui Neng*. See Price and Wong 1969, part II, pp. 11–12.

4. This point is made repeatedly in the Buddha's teachings. See, for example, *Dhammapada* v.44–45. and 103–105.

5. See the Larger Sutra on Amitayus, the Longer *Sukhavativyuha Sutra*. The Pure Land Sutras have been translated and extensively commented upon by Hisao Inagaki.

6. The name Dharmakara means one for whom the Dharma is their fixed purpose in life. There is a probably intentional parallel between this name and the word *samskara* which indicates having the mind fixed to things other than Dharma.

7. In chapter one of the Vimalakirti Sutra we are told that the spirit of the bodhisattva path beginning with wholeheartedness is the pure land. See the translation by Burton Watson published by Columbia University Press (1997) pp. 26–30.

Chapter Twenty-Four: *Right Action*

1. Or, we could say, they are contained by the grace of Amida which is within and all around us. It is this sense of the omnipresence of this saving power that makes Buddhism a religion. This should not, however, be thought of as something supernatural, but rather as a dramatic way of describing one of the basic laws of the universe. This is not magic. It is simply the way reality works.

Chapter Twenty-Five: *Right Livelihood*

1. Yelui lived 1189–1243.
2. Jiyu Kennett, *Zen Is Eternal Life*, Dharma Publishing (1976), p. 160.
3. The progressively increasing divorce between the activities of life in modern society and their intended ends was perceived and elegantly documented by the sociologist Georg Simmel who pointed out how this trend leads to an atrophy of the capacity for acts of will. See Peter Lawrence's translations of selections from Simmel's work, *Georg Simmel, Sociologist and European*, published by Nelson (1976), especially the section called 'The Style of Life' on pages 173–221

Chapter Twenty-Six: *Right Effort*

1. This saying by the Korean Dhyana Master Kusan is reported by R. E. Buswell in *The Zen Monastic Experience*, published by Princeton University Press (1992).
2. *Anguttara Nikaya 6.55*.
3. 'You are a mortal man ... today you live, and tomorrow you are dust; one fever will quench your pride': spoken by Romanus, emperor of Constantinople to the invading Bulgarian king Symeon. See, D. Obolensky, *The Byzantine Commonwealth*. London: Cardinal(1974), p. 153
4. Zen Master Nhat Hanh, in a lecture given at Plum Village, France, in September 1996, suggested that we should translate the term *ksanti* by the word 'capacity' since it indicates our capacity to cope with the vicissitudes of life in a constructive way.

Chapter Twenty-Seven: *Right Mindfulness*

1. *Namo Amida Buddha* literally means 'I call upon (or I take refuge in) the Buddha of Infinite Light'. Sometimes it is said *na-mo-a-mi-da-bu*' with just six syllables. *Om Mani Padme Hum* is all but untranslatable. A rough rendering would be 'hail to the jewel in the lotus', but with these phrases what is important is the stringing together of a number of individual words or syllables each of which has a wealth of resonance and association. Many other mantras exist, each generally associated with the invocation of one of the many figures who, in Buddhism, personify the qualities of enlightenment and help us realise them in ourselves. For simplicity, the discussion in this book has been limited to Amida and Quan Yin, two of the best known and most loved.

Chapter Twenty-Eight: *Right Samadhi*

1. The Visualisation Sutra is one of the Pure Land Sutras already referred to in note 5 to chapter 23.
2. H. Inagaki, *The Three Pure Land Sutras*, published by Nagata Bunshodo (1994), p. 320.

Chapter Thirty: *Conclusion*

1. The name the Buddha used for himself is *Tathagata*. Opinions vary about its correct translation. I have taken it as implying 'been there' but it could equally mean 'thus gone', though what the implication of the latter term might have been in the context of his time is guesswork.

Bibliography

Batchelor, S. (1983) *Alone With Others*. New York: Grove Press.

Brazier, D.J. (editor) (1993) *Beyond Carl Rogers*, London: Constable.

Brazier, D J. (1995) *Zen Therapy*. London: Constable.

Buswell, R.E. (1992) *The Zen Monastic Experience*. New Jersey: Princeton University Press.

Cleary, T. (1990) *Transmission of Light*. San Francisco: North Point Press.

Cleary, T. (1993) *No Barrier: Unlocking the Zen Koan*. London: HarperCollins.

Easwaran, E. (1987) *The Dhammapada*. London: Arkana.

Freud, S. (1924) 'The ecomonic problem of masochism'. *On Metapsychology*. London: Penguin, pp.409–426.

Hanh, N. (1990) *Transformation and Healing*. Berkeley: Parallax.

Hanh, N. (1975/1991) *Miracle of Mindfulness*. London: Rider.

Hanh, N. (1992) *The Diamod that Cuts Through Illusion*. Berkeley: Parallax.

Hanh, N. (1993) *Thundering Silence: Sutra on knowing the better way to catch a snake*. Berkeley: Parallax.

Hanh, N. (1993a) *The Blooming of a Lotus: Guided meditation exercises for healing and transformation*. Boston: Beacon Press.

Hanh, N. (1993b) *The Blooming of a Lotus*. Boston: Beacon Press.

Hopkins, J. (1983) *Meditation on Emptiness*. London: Wisdom.

Inagaki, H. (1994) *The Three Pure Land Sutras*. Kyoto: Nagata Bunshodo.

Isigami, Z. (1989) *Disciples of the Buddha*. Tokyo: Kosei.

Kennett, J. (1976) *Zen Is Eternal Life*. Emeryville, California: Dharma Publishing.

Khantipalo (1964) *Tolerance: A study from Buddhist sources*. London: Rider.

Kornfield, J. (1994) *A Path with Heart*. London: Rider.

Kwee, M.G.T. (editor) (1990) *Psychotherapy, Meditation and Health*. London: East-West Publications.

Lawrence, P. (1976) *Georg Simmel, Sociologist and European*. Sunbury, Middlesex: Nelson.

Li, R. (1993) *The Biographical Scripture of King Ashoka*. Berkeley: Numata Centre.

Macy, J. (1983) *Despair and Personal Power in the Nuclear Age*. Philadelphia: New Society Publishers.

Manné, B.J. (1992) *Debates and Case Histories in the Pali Canon*. Doctoral thesis presented to University of Utrecht.

Marris, P. (1986) *Loss and Change*. London: Routledge & Kegan Paul.

Mascaro, J. (1973) *The Dhammapada: The Path of Freedom*. London: Penguin.

Moreno, J.L. (1934) *Who Shall Survive*. Washington, DC: Nervous and Mental Disease Publishing Co.

Nanananda Bhikkhu (1973) *Ideal Solitude*. Kandy, Sri Lanka: Buddhist Publication Society.

Narada (1973) *The Buddha and his Teachings*. Singapore Buddhist Meditation Centre.

Nyanaponika Thera (1974) *The Snake Simile*. Kandy, Sri Lanka: Buddhist Publication Society.

Obolensky, D. (1974) *The Byzantine Commonwealth*. London: Cardinal.

Okamura, S. (translator) (1987) *Shobogenzo-zuimonki: Sayings of Eihei dogen Zenji recorded by Koun Ejo*. Kyoto: Kyoto Soto Zen Centre.

Parkes, C.M. (1972) *Bereavement: Studies of grief in adult life*. New York: International Universities Press.

Payutto, P.A. (1994) *Dependent Origination: The Buddhist law of conditionality*. Bangkok: Buddhadhamma Foundation.

Phuong, C.N. (1993) *Learning True Love*. Berkeley: Parallax.

Price, A.F. & Wong, M.L. (translators) (1969) *The Diamond Sutra and the Sutra of Hui Neng*. Boston: Shambhala.

Rahula, W. (1959–1978) *What the Buddha Taught.* London: Gordon Fraser.

Reps, P. (1957) *Zen Flesh, Zen Bones.* London: Penguin.

Rogers, C.R. (1957) 'The necessary and sufficient conditions of therapeutic personality change'. *Journal of Consulting Psychology 21,* 95–103.

Rogers, C.R. (1980) *A Way of Being.* Boston: Houghton Mifflin.

Scheff, T J. (1979) *Catharsis, Healing, Ritual and Drama.* Berkeley: University of California Press.

Sekida, K. (1977) *Two Zen Classics.* New York: Weatherhill.

Sekida, K. (1985) *Zen Training: Methods and Philosophy.* New York: Weatherhill.

Shay, J. (1994) *Achilles in Vietnam: Combat trauma and the undoing of character.* New York: Simon & Schuster.

Stryk, L. (1995) *The Awakened Self: Encounters with Zen.* New York: Kodansha International.

Suzuki, D. T. (1950) *Essays in Zen Buddhism (Second Series).* London: Rider.

Suzuki, S. (1970) *Zen Mind Beginner's Mind.* New York: Weatherhill.

Tanahashi, K. & Schneider, T.D. (1994) *Essential Zen.* London: HarperCollins.

Taylor, D. (1996) *The Healing Power of Stories.* Dublin: Gill & Macmillan.

Thien-an (1975) *Zen Philosophy Zen Practice.* Berkeley: Dharma Publishing.

Trungpa, C. (1987) *Cutting Through Spiritual Materialism.* London: Shambhala.

Watson, B. (1997) *The Vimalakirti Sutra.* New York: Columbia University Press.

Watts, A.W. (1957) *The Way of Zen.* London: Penguin.

Worden, J.W. (1983–1988) *Grief Counselling and Grief Therapy.* London: Routledge.

Index